Poems From The East
Edited by Vivien Linton

First published in Great Britain in 2008 by:
Young Writers
Remus House
Coltsfoot Drive
Peterborough
PE2 9JX
Telephone: 01733 890066
Website: www.youngwriters.co.uk

All Rights Reserved

© Copyright Contributors 2008

SB ISBN 978-1 84431 743 1

Foreword

Young Writers' Big Green Poetry Machine is a showcase for our nation's most brilliant young poets to share their thoughts, hopes and fears for the planet they call home.

Young Writers was established in 1990 to nurture creativity in our children and young adults, to give them an interest in poetry and an outlet to express themselves. Seeing their work in print will encourage them to keep writing as they grow, and become our poets of tomorrow.

Selecting the poems has been challenging and immensely rewarding. The effort and imagination invested by these young writers makes their poems a pleasure to enjoy reading time and time again.

Contents

Barnabas Oley CE Primary School, Sandy
Sophia Abbasi (11)	1
Tara Jefferies (10)	1
James Ellison (11)	2
Matthew Greenland (10)	2
Ottilie Black (11)	3
Tom Kennedy (11)	3
Alice Howie (10)	4
Leo Penrose (10)	4
John Taylor (10)	5
Joshua Wilson (10)	5
Shannon Coppen (10)	6
Beth Holmes (10)	6
Lucy Huckle (11)	6
Robert Holmes (10)	7

Bedford Preparatory School, Bedford
David Hickey (10)	7
Robert Salvesen (9)	7
Max Thackara (9)	8
Nicholas Stalley (10)	8
Adam Johnston & Benjamin Poslad (10)	9
Dexter Southern & James Brodrip (10)	9
Samuel Holland & Oliver Meniru (10)	10

Brampton Village Primary School, Huntingdon
Abigail Bleakley (10)	10
Mica Covell (10)	11
Bromwyn Holland (10)	11
Jannike Smye (10)	12
Hannah Stanley (10)	12
Megan Hill (10)	13
Chloé Hornby (9)	13
David Oliver & Freta (10)	14
Amy Natasha Smith (10)	14
Lucie Selwyn (9) & Chantelle Martley (10)	14
Emelia Brown (10)	15
Anna Hyde (10)	15
Tom Coggin (10)	16

Alex Connor (10)	16
Matthew Pickering (10)	16
Ross Puckey (9)	17
Jake Muff (10)	17
Alysia Phoenix (11)	18
Evie Belgrove (10)	18
Alex Lambton (10)	19
Max Bradshaw-Clifford (10)	19
Harry Clarke (10)	19
Sophie Clark (11)	20
Charlie Mercer (9)	20
Jonny Charalambous (10)	21
Néve Richards (10)	21
Alice Dines-Allen (11)	22
Ben Stevenson (11)	22

Bromham CE Lower School, Bedford

Louise Kiddy (8)	23
Hannah Cornwell (8)	23
Megan Clayton (8)	24
Jack Tilling (8)	24
Taylor Bland (9)	25
Charles Pope (9)	25
Lauren Tolmie (8)	25
Kristie Prew (9)	26
Jamie Banghard (9)	26
Natasha Smiljanic (8)	26
Selena Quambusch (9)	27
Conna Lenihan (9)	27
Tommy Hardwick (9)	27
Chiara Demichele (8)	28
Harry Gray (8)	28
Danesh Sundar (9)	28
Samuel Tredray (9)	29
Kayley-Ann Freame (8)	29
Ethan Green (7)	29
Alex Taylor (8)	30
Dan Franklin (8)	30
Emily Stanton (8)	30
Laura Dwyer (8)	31
Ellis Bell (8)	31

Silas Atherton (8)	31
Katie Davis (8)	32
Jessica Rowlett (8)	32
Eloise Peacock (7)	32
Sonia Sundar (7)	33
Dani May Shaw (8)	33
Gemma Ware (8)	34
Kirsty Krzywopulski (9)	34
Molly McCarthy (8)	35
Madeline O'Neill (8)	35
Adam Cook (8)	35
Ellie Adams (7)	36
Lauryn Peart (8)	36
Jacob Cientanni (8)	36
Scarlett Ash-Ingley (8)	37
Isabel Filby (7)	37
George Kelly (8)	37
Eleanor-Rose Bown (8)	38
Jake Webster (8)	38
Joshua Spencer (8)	39
Mason Ludovico (8)	39
Lauren Butterworth (8)	39
Holly Fisher (7)	40
Joshua Gibson (8)	40
Joshua Hands (7)	41
Sophie Latoo (8)	41
George Morris (8)	41
Toby Haggerwood (8)	42
Beau Rodd (8)	42
Joshua White (8)	42
Oliver Litchfield (8)	43
Sam Perkins (8)	43
Kieran White (8)	43
Jack Wheatley (8)	44
Emily Fleming (8)	44
Charie Hislop (8)	44
Sophie Nixon (8)	45
Skye Haggith (7)	45
Rachel Fish (8)	45

Dallow Primary School, Luton
Dalziel Holder (9) — 46
Daniel Fedorov (9) — 46
Mohammed Humza Raja (10) — 46
Hamad Jamil (9) — 47
Ameena Hussain (11) — 47
Halimah Isbag (11) — 47
Monwara Bibi (9) — 48
Abid Ahmed & Samiun Rahman (10) — 48
Shakil Ahmed & Abu-Sayeed Miah (10) — 48
Rohima Nessa & Anisa Khan (10) — 49

Elm Road Primary School, Wisbech
Neve Gordon-Farleigh (8) — 49
Grace Cherry (8) — 49
Mia Churchill (8) — 50

Holmer Green Junior School, Holmer Green
Niamh Murdoch (9) — 50
Jacob Pompe (9) — 50
Jamie Brazier (10) — 51
Robert Huw Bagley (11) — 51
Hannah May Leonard (10) — 52
Vicki Tutt (10) — 52
Fiona Hollings (11) — 53
Shaun Jillians (9) — 53
Cameron Garden (11) — 54
Emma Cooper (10) — 54
Catherine Kirby (11) — 55
Mason Wright (11) — 55

Maltman's Green School, Gerrards Cross
Verity Hunn (9) — 56
Pippa Nester (8) — 56
Jenna Arnot (7) — 57
Ellie Green (8) — 57
Victoria Taylor (11) — 58
Milly Trenwith (8) — 58
Rebecca Sillett (10) — 59
Emily Lue-Fong (7) — 59

Gagan Grewal (10)	60
Annicke Van Wyk (7)	60
Jemima Lomax (10)	61
Louise Thomassin (8)	61
Charlotte Williams (10)	62
Eleanor Thornton (8)	62
Sophia Scott (10)	63
Annabelle Corfield (8)	63
Georgia Bingham (10)	64
Madeleine Champion (8)	64

Queen Edith Primary School, Cambridge

Jibril Rashid (11)	65
Daniel Turner (11)	65
Natalia Rogowska (11)	66
Phoebe Wheeler (11)	67
Anthea Chui (11)	68
Natalia de la Cueva (11)	70
Holly Hayes (11)	71
William Sharp (11)	72
Cristina D'Uva (11)	73
Puja Chudasama (11)	74
Joseph Fallon (11)	75
Rhian Hughes (11)	76

St Alban's Catholic Primary School, Cambridge

Eleanor Wager & Ellen Wallwork (8)	77
Megan Meredith-Rodriguez (9)	77
Ellen Curran & Graciela (9)	78
Saskia Capetti (9)	78
Aisling Munnelly (8)	79
Sean-Francis Calvey (9)	79

St Joseph's Junior School, Luton

Pauline Mwakulegwa (11)	80
Daniel Staniforth (11)	80
Emily Godfrey (11)	81
Joe Grossi & Jordan West (11)	82
Ben Murray (11)	82
Jessica Gajewski (11)	83
Thomas Mayne (11)	83

Amber Hutton (11)   84
Niamh Timmons McCullagh (10)   84
Tiarnan Doherty (11)   85
Thulani Ncube (11)   85
Kinga Nawrocka (11)   86

Stanton School, Milton Keynes
Lien Fox   86
Kirston Woods (10)   86
Christopher Arnold (11)   87
Sasha Stoker-Jackson (11)   87
Shelby Fuller (10)   88
Rachael Wayman (10)   88
Courtenay Wooding (11)   89
Lisa Ann Waite (11)   89
Rachel Dosunmu (11)   90
Cara Brooker (11)   90
Iman Mohammed (10)   91
Haseeb Ahmad Syed (11)   91
Samantha Masedza (11)   92
Suheub Awale (11)   92
Shannon Griffin (11)   93
Kayleigh-Louise Wills (11)   93
Ankur Vaghadia (11)   94
Ali Ul-Zafar (11)   94
George Wilson (11)   95
Stephanie Takyi (10)   95

Sundon Park Junior School, Luton
Ben Scott (9)   96
Samantha Thompson (10)   96
Samamtha Cox (9)   97
Sophie Little (9)   97
Ross Grieves (9)   98
Charlotte Rattigan (9)   98
Kyle Perry (10)   99
Regan Cook (9)   99
Sophie Allford-Rowe (9)   100
Destiny-Blu Atkinson (9)   100
Luke Chambers (10)   101
Elisabeth Bunker (10)   101

Ellisse-Renais Clarke (9)	102
Bethany Ruck (9)	102
Matthew Wajda (9)	102
Aidan Drury (9)	103
Sophie Mullings (10)	103
Ryan O'Reilly (10)	103
Luke Williams (8)	104
Danielle Fortune (9)	104

Welland Primary School, Peterborough

Crystal Bonnar (11) & Kara Watkin	105
Jasmine May House (11)	105
Chloe Nickelson (10) & Shannon Mouatt (11)	106

William Austin Junior School, Luton

Awais Riaz (8)	106
Habibur Rahman (9)	106
Keira Chew (9)	107
Sumayyah Iqbal (9)	107
Sabia Shafiq (9)	107
Arooj Khan (9)	108
Georgia Webster (9)	108
Chloe Walker (9)	109
Alina Ali (8)	109

The Poems

On My Way To School

On my way to school I hear
The brrmm of the car engine,
The chatter of my siblings,
All the birds as they fly and sing,
The ducks and the geese
And the bumps in the road as the car goes over these.
I see the sun shining, the shadow of the trees
And the leaves shaking because of the breeze.
The school drive grows nearer,
I see the car of my teacher,
We park the car and walk the rest of the way
This is because I live far away.

We walk across a few streets
Say hello to the people we meet
This is a very fun way
To help *save* the planet.

Sophia Abbasi (11)
Barnabas Oley CE Primary School, Sandy

Listen As The Earth Goes Round

Drip-drop, pitter-patter
The rain trickles down
Shine, shine, dusty gold
The sun is coming out!
Chirp, chirp, tweet, tweet
Flying, swooping birds
Honk, honk, beep, beep
A car passes by.
Pit-pat, pit-pat
My feet walk through the puddles
I reach the school
I listen, I listen, I listen as the Earth goes round.

Tara Jefferies (10)
Barnabas Oley CE Primary School, Sandy

While Walking

While walking on my way to school I heard . . .
A little bird,
A pigeon call
And the kick of a football.

With all these lovely things
Why is there need for a tractor
Or trucks
Forcing animals into nooks?

Oil power is wrecking us
So why not use the bus?
Do you like what you are seeing?
The world is damaged by human beings.

James Ellison (11)
Barnabas Oley CE Primary School, Sandy

Climate Change

I hear a bird sing
And a bicycle ring.
I can hear a car from long range,
It's the cause of climate change.
The wind blows in my face,
It's the end of the human race.
I see the recycle man
Recycling a baked bean can.
The world will end,
It's round the bend
But we will stop the smoke,
So we don't choke.

Matthew Greenland (10)
Barnabas Oley CE Primary School, Sandy

On My Way To School

On my way to school I hear . . .
Babies shrieking,
Birds tweeting,
Bees buzzing,
And car horns beeping.

On my way to school I see . . .
The sun shining,
The trees swaying
And my best friend waiting for me by the school gate.

On my way to school I feel . . .
The wind blowing a slight breeze through my hair,
The long grass brushing against my leg,
Now I'm ready for a new school day.

Ottilie Black (11)
Barnabas Oley CE Primary School, Sandy

Walking To School

Walking to school
I heard the engines of the cars
I saw the car wasn't far.

Walking to school
I heard children talking to their mum
I saw some people looking glum.

Walking to school
I heard the birds tweet
I saw lots of people in the street.

Tom Kennedy (11)
Barnabas Oley CE Primary School, Sandy

Walking To School

Walking to school I heard . . .
A rabbit bounce,
A cat pounce
And my dog's collar jingle.
I heard the trees rustle
The cars hustle
And the people walk on by.
But there's one thing that caught my eye
The whole world in its beauty.
I felt the sun bearing down on my back
And the wind blowing me off track.
I saw the sky so clear it was crystal-blue
There was just the sun there which gave me a clue, it was summer!
I smelt the flowers as I walked and saw
This is the world I was born for.
And this is what happened when I walked to school.

Alice Howie (10)
Barnabas Oley CE Primary School, Sandy

Walking To School Each Day

Walking to school each day, I hear the birdies say
'This is my place and you are a disgrace!
All our cars polluting the world when I just fly, wings uncurled.'
The rustling of trees and the bumblebees
I feel the cold wind on my leg
A bike goes by, it is my friend Greg.
Cars and vans are a no-no thing
But walking and cycling makes your body feel a ting!
Buses are better, they mean less car journeys
But walking is the best so walk if you please.

Leo Penrose (10)
Barnabas Oley CE Primary School, Sandy

Walking To School

As I walk to school each day
I hear the birdies all the way,
But all the cars come up the street
As I hear feet.
The wind blows
And a light glows.

I see the creatures of the world looking down at me,
I can also see
Cars and noises all around,
Never stop, never frown.
I feel the cool breeze in my hair
As I carry my bag, life's so unfair.

John Taylor (10)
Barnabas Oley CE Primary School, Sandy

Walking To School

Walking to school each day
I hear the wind blowing,
I see lights glowing,
I feel the ground vibrate,
I think it may be an earthquake.
When I arrive at school
I see mums talking,
I hear feet walking,
I feel water on my face
But there is no rain
Instead there is a hurricane!

Joshua Wilson (10)
Barnabas Oley CE Primary School, Sandy

Walking To School I Heard . . .

Walking to school I heard leaves rustling, trees swaying.
I saw people talking, people walking.
I felt the cool breeze on my knobbly knees.
I smelt blossoming flowers for hours and hours
But there's more, I heard my cat's bell jingle and the doorbells ringing.
My feet were burning whilst wheels were turning.
But there's one more thing I need to know, that's why the world
                                          just glows and glows.

Shannon Coppen (10)
Barnabas Oley CE Primary School, Sandy

Think!

Pollution is a horrid thing, we hear it in the news.
When cars zoom by they don't really know how much petrol
                                          they really use.
As I wait for the bus every single day and listen to the birds
They try to sing but are covered up by cars going round the bends.
The countryside is full of trees with the wind rustling their leaves.
Sadly, they're cut down in winter to be our Christmas trees.
Think, listen and stop pollution.

Beth Holmes (10)
Barnabas Oley CE Primary School, Sandy

Walking To School

Walking to school
I hear the *tweet tweet* of the birds
And the loud noises of the cars.
I feel the cool breeze on my face,
And the warm sun on my back.
I see the trees rustling and people bustling.
All around me, it's a chaotic world.

Lucy Huckle (11)
Barnabas Oley CE Primary School, Sandy

Walking To School

Walking to school when
I heard a bird sing,
I saw cars and lorries,
I felt the cool breeze in my hair
And I smelt the fresh air.

Robert Holmes (10)
Barnabas Oley CE Primary School, Sandy

Fairtrade

F eed the poor and stop poverty
A nimals must be treated fairly or they will become extinct
I solate chucking rubbish around
R ecycle all your pots and tins
T each the world to love and care
R acism must be stopped
A ntarctica's ice will be no more
D istraction and wars must be stopped
E veryone must follow these rules to make the world a better place.

David Hickey (10)
Bedford Preparatory School, Bedford

Recycle

R ecycle all your pots and tins
E lse the world will come to an end
C old ice caps will start to melt
Y oung children will not see the wonders that we have
C an't you see it's destroying our world?
L ots of animals will lose their homes in the rainforests
E veryone must make an effort.

Robert Salvesen (9)
Bedford Preparatory School, Bedford

Litter Me Timbers

Why is litter
Such a thing in the world?
It is so very bitter,
So why is there litter?

You can find it in London
Cambridge or Bedford,
Litter is everywhere
So it cannot be ignored.

Litter me timbers
What do you say?
There's more of it now,
It's not drifting away.

Let's do something about it,
Let's clear up the streets.
Come on, let's go,
Let's not stamp our feet.

Now we have done it
Doesn't it look nice?
We have done it now
It's not crawling with mice.

Max Thackara (9)
Bedford Preparatory School, Bedford

Recycle

R educe, reuse, recycle
E lectricity must be turned off if you aren't in the room, don't
C ut down the trees. Use the
Y ellowy-orange bags to recycle paper etc.
C hange the world or
L oads of animals will start dying. Use
E nergy-efficient lightbulbs and save the world.

Nicholas Stalley (10)
Bedford Preparatory School, Bedford

The Environment

Make the world
A better place
Or your children
Will be in disgrace.

Recycle all your paper
And do not do it later.
Do not drive each day
Cycle to help the world.

Don't start dropping litter
Or things will be quite bitter.

Do what you've been told
Stand up, *yes,* be bold!

Save the world.

Adam Johnston & Benjamin Poslad (10)
Bedford Preparatory School, Bedford

The Fumes

The fumes roll out day by day
I wish they could go away.
Pollution travel across the air
Why does it have to be so unfair?
Do the animals have to die?
It just makes me want to cry.
The ozone layer gets even thinner,
It makes us even dimmer.
Global warming kills off life
It makes much, much more than strife.

So everyone, you need to help!

Dexter Southern & James Brodrip (10)
Bedford Preparatory School, Bedford

The Young Man From Beijing

There was a young man from Beijing
Who did not have a recycling bin.
He went out of his way
To buy one that day.
And his rubbish he always put in.

There was a man's brain that went *ping*
He had realised he didn't have a recycling bin.
So he went out of his way
To buy one that day
But he could still use his old dustbin.

Samuel Holland & Oliver Meniru (10)
Bedford Preparatory School, Bedford

The Rainforest

I am the rainforest, please listen to me,
I want to protest cos you're killing me,
You're cutting me down and burning me.
I want to live as much as you do
And I bet you wouldn't like it if I was killing you!
First go my trees leaving my birds homeless,
Then goes my soil being nutrient drained,
I'm dying fast so help me please.
I hold so many things both animals and plants,
Show you care, don't pollute the air!
I need a lot of love, animals and all that's there,
Killing them all for all you care!
So please, please, please help me,
I want to live, my life has value
So help me, do what you can,
You know you can, stop deforestation!

Abigail Bleakley (10)
Brampton Village Primary School, Huntingdon

Save The Rainforests

S ave the animals of the rainforest
A nd stop being greedy
V iolent bulldozers flatten the land
E veryone needs to help save the trees.

T he tropical tiger is becoming extinct
H elp them quickly
E very animal of the rainforest is very important.

R aging machines eat away at the land
A cre after acre is destroyed.
I nfinite numbers of trees are destroyed every minute
N ever to be seen again
F orever it is gone
O ver the years more and more have disappeared
R ainforest species vanishing fast
E very insect counts
S top deforestation now!
T oo many trees are destroyed each year
S top deforestation, we have to act now!

Mica Covell (10)
Brampton Village Primary School, Huntingdon

Rainforest

R emember if you're cutting down the trees, you're killing
    animals' homes.
A nimals are dying every single second
I 'm not very happy with the amount of trees being cut down
N ow show that you care by not cutting trees down
F rightened animals are scared of their homes being destroyed
O ther than that, stop deforestation now!
R escue the animals, trees, plants and the Amazon river
E xtinction means that you're hurting yourself and soon the world
S o save the damage you've done and replace them with new,
T o save the world, stop cutting down trees and destroying
    the animals' homes and save the world.

Bromwyn Holland (10)
Brampton Village Primary School, Huntingdon

Save The Rainforest

S top deforestation, you're only being selfish
A nimals are endangered because mankind doesn't care
V icious chainsaws chopping away the life
E xtinction's on the way mankind, so beware!

T rees provide the oxygen that keeps us all alive
H ummingbirds, small they may be, but
E very bird is as important as thee!

R avenous humans
A ttack helpless trees
I n vain, they wipe away all the life.
N asty bulldozers clearing the land, while
F ierce fighting frogs charge in battle!
O h but if plants are destroyed what will the herbivores eat?
R ainforest, then can't help them
E xtinction's on the way mankind
S o save
T he rainforest.

Jannike Smye (10)
Brampton Village Primary School, Huntingdon

A Croc's Point Of View

Oh how lovely, a pair of boots in a shop
Too bad they were made from an innocent croc!
Many animals suffer from pain
But nobody cares with the profits Man can gain.
Lots of mankind are catered for
But what about us? They've not thought of us before.
You are slowly killing off me and my prey
But some day you will pay.
Captured animals are put in harsh conditions
While pet traders accomplish their missions.
People can get very greedy
But can't they see that crocs too are needy?

Hannah Stanley (10)
Brampton Village Primary School, Huntingdon

The Rainforest

Night breaks into day
You can see the horizon rising in a colourful purple mist
Apes in the trees
Apes fighting and using their fists
Rain falls silently
After, the water looks like diamonds shining, glittering in the sun
The waterfall falls swiftly
 Monkeys playing in the waterfall, it looks like fun
Something has happened
Something has happened overnight, more trees are gone
Someone has been here
People have been here, they've destroyed our homes, we're going,
                                                                                                    they've won!

Tropical plants
Many rare plants are dying here
Amazing animals
'Help us,' hear the cries of many animals that have died here,
                                                                                                                     feel their fear

Good day
For us it is not a good day
Save us now, we're disappearing so help us *today!*

Megan Hill (10)
Brampton Village Primary School, Huntingdon

The Rainforest

The bright sun lights the horizon faster than a cheetah can run
The trees are cut down, their trunks are dark brown
Monkeys in the canopy and emergent swinging up and down fall
Because they've just cut a tree down
Water falls, water falls down
It makes a splash when it hits the cold ground
Animals die, the birds may still fly to the sky
So save the beautiful tropical land of the rainforest
We will save it together.

Chloé Hornby (9)
Brampton Village Primary School, Huntingdon

Save Our Animals

We are the animals of the rainforest, its survival that we are fighting for
Many tigers are dying; we must save the tigers soon.
Selfish Man killing tigers for their skin,
Man makes money, tiger becomes extinct.

The hummingbird will hum no more for Man will destroy their home.
If Man stands in their way, they will fade away.

So you see, the animals plead
Leave our homes now for next *you'll* be extinct!

David Oliver & Freta (10)
Brampton Village Primary School, Huntingdon

Animals

A live we were but suffering now
N ever will we survive without our homes
I n life we've had good times years ago
M aybe you could save us but it will be hard
A ll of us want a happy life but not now, it's war
L ife is hard when no one helps
S ave us now, please, please, please, save us now.

Amy Natasha Smith (10)
Brampton Village Primary School, Huntingdon

The Jaguars' Jaws

J aguars' jaws crunching into other animals' bodies
A nimals screeching to get away
G reedy men killing poor jaguars
U gly women wearing jaguars' coats
A ngry jaguars becoming extinct
R unning as fast as they can go from the hunters.

Lucie Selwyn (9) & Chantelle Martley (10)
Brampton Village Primary School, Huntingdon

The Rainforest Destruction

The rainforest is a noisy scorching place
Where animals roam and predators chase
The trees grow high
Up into the light blue sky
And the birds flap their feathered wings.

The trees of the canopy have swinging monkeys
Swooping through the branches, big and chunky
But in the distance you can hear the arrival of a machine
Tearing the bushes into little parts of green
And cutting down trees in its path.

Fifty years from now there could be not much to see
All the animals in captivity
Destruction, deforestation all around
No more trees, no more bushes on the ground.

So listen, listen, I hope you agree,
That saving the rainforest is down to you and me.

Emelia Brown (10)
Brampton Village Primary School, Huntingdon

Rainforests

R ain is falling on the treetops
A nimals are losing their homes every day
I nsects are creeping around on the forest floor
N ever take animals out of their home
F or a long time the animals have been wild and free
O xygen is running low
R oaring lions
E choing noise across the land
S ome people don't know what they are doing
T rees are being cut down every day
S ave our rainforest.

Anna Hyde (10)
Brampton Village Primary School, Huntingdon

Rainforest

R ainforests
A re getting cut down
I ndigenous tribes are losing their homes
N obody should chop down trees
F orests must be saved
O rang-utans are being killed
R ain is polluted with acid
E verything is getting destroyed
S ave the animals
T hey are in danger.

Tom Coggin (10)
Brampton Village Primary School, Huntingdon

Monkey Madness

M onkeys in the treetops
O n a beautiful day
N o, it can't be
K nowing we've got to go
E veryone, run!
Y es, mankind is here
S o they cut down our trees for their satisfaction.

Alex Connor (10)
Brampton Village Primary School, Huntingdon

The Toucan On Strike

I'm bright, I'm colourful,
I'm becoming extinct
So save me now or I'll
Be gone in a blink!
I'm wonderful, I'm scared,
I'm losing my home
So stop the destruction, *go, go, go!*

Matthew Pickering (10)
Brampton Village Primary School, Huntingdon

Rainforest - Haikus

The rainforest holds
Many animals and trees
Blowing in the breeze.

Please don't cut trees down
For the safety of humans
Please don't cut trees down.

No one wants to die
But you're putting us in sight
Of dying by fright.

I know you are poor
I know you need money but
Stop cutting trees down.

Please stop killing us
For everybody also
For yourselves, please stop!

Ross Puckey (9)
Brampton Village Primary School, Huntingdon

The Rainforest

The trees,
The bees,
The wildlife is dying
And the birds are flying
Away, away from their homes.

Pollution in the air
Poverty everywhere.
We need to stop this
We cannot miss
Pollution causes smoke
And if we don't we choke!

Jake Muff (10)
Brampton Village Primary School, Huntingdon

Small Dog

I have been abandoned today,
My owner does not like me and my doggy friends.
I have been shouted at all day today,
I have starved today, no meat, no nothing.

My owner hated me,
The children promised not to leave me,
Nobody liked me.
Their cat nearly ate me!
Because I am so small I can't do a lot of things.

I've lost my fur,
I cannot bark or howl.
I'm so heartbroken,
I've been left for weeks,
You can see my ribs I'm so hungry.

Alysia Phoenix (11)
Brampton Village Primary School, Huntingdon

Rainforests

R ain is falling on the emergent layer every day
A s the birds fly, animals die
I n come lumberjacks
N ow stop!
F orest floor packed with insects
O thers don't care
R acing snakes slither fast
E choes spread as
S uddenly a bang from
T rees falling
S o please save our rainforest.

Evie Belgrove (10)
Brampton Village Primary School, Huntingdon

Poor Rainforest Animals

Why is life so difficult to handle?
For animals of a rainforest, it is now in a mangle.
Even though amazing creatures we are
Has the time come for our homes to become tar?
Where does our home go?
Is it those hairless things who see us as low?
They shoot us, they skin us,
I wonder what they see, a pathetic bit of fuzz?
Life was fine till those abominators came along
Heartless, cruel, we have endured it too long.
The deadly creatures are as aggressive as they look.

Alex Lambton (10)
Brampton Village Primary School, Huntingdon

Jaguar

J aguars' jagged jaws crunching on their prey
A nimals screeching to get away
G iant polluting air destroying the animals and their habitats
U seful fruit saves animals' lives and habitats
A cid rain burning animals and destroying animals' habitats
R oaring jaguars screeching to find juicy prey.

Max Bradshaw-Clifford (10)
Brampton Village Primary School, Huntingdon

Untitled

Save us, the toucans
Please do not cut down our trees
Help us to survive
We are really sad
Because our homes are destroyed
Please help us live now!

Harry Clarke (10)
Brampton Village Primary School, Huntingdon

My Last Prayer

I've been lying here
Since yesterday
He picked me up
I just wanted to play.

He rushed me away
In the dead of night
I was put in a car
With not a single light.

I'm ever so parched
Not even a scrap
The demon that pinched me
Wore a filthy brown cap.

He hit me, he whipped me
He won't let me go
I wonder if my sadness
I'll ever show.

I don't know my future
I'm not in good care
This is to you Ted
I gave you my last prayer.

Sophie Clark (11)
Brampton Village Primary School, Huntingdon

Rainforest

R unning rain falling from the sky
A nimals in the trees that are so high
I n the rainforest the lumberjack is mean
N ature is to be seen
F orest floor where trees are landing
O n snakes and spiders
R ain is making muddy puddles, so
E ach animal is mad
S o the animals say, 'We want to have our homes back.
T oday!'

Charlie Mercer (9)
Brampton Village Primary School, Huntingdon

The Poor Dog

The dog just sat there
With his long scruffy hair
Waiting for his owner to return
The pain in his stomach just churns

The dog just sat there
With his long scruffy hair
Waiting for some food
In a very bad mood

The dog just sat there
With his long scruffy hair
He realised the owner left him
With a hurt limb

The dog just sat there
With his long scruffy hair
You can help.

Jonny Charalambous (10)
Brampton Village Primary School, Huntingdon

Save Our Rainforest

We make lots of acid rain
We put animals through lots of pain.

Parrots live up on the trees
But when they fly down there are no bees.

The people who live in the town
Every day they cut trees down.

Because we cause CO_2
There is something we must do.

So save our rainforest
Not just today but every day.

Néve Richards (10)
Brampton Village Primary School, Huntingdon

The Tearful Dog

You think I'm sweet
And very neat,
They think I'm old
And don't do what I'm told.

My owners chucked me out
With a cry and a shout
And now I'm alone
Sleeping on the grubby stone.

You think I'm small
And very cool
They think I'm strong
But they've got it all wrong.

And now I am weak
I can't stand on my feet,
I've got nowhere to go
And I can't go home.

Alice Dines-Allen (11)
Brampton Village Primary School, Huntingdon

The Chained Dog

My owner has abandoned me
He's gone home for his tea.
He's left me alone
Without a bone.

I am really thirsty
I'm begging for mercy.
I'm really bored
So I pray to the Lord.

I've been lying here for a day
And I want to play.
Everyone rushing by
Leaving me to die.

Ben Stevenson (11)
Brampton Village Primary School, Huntingdon

I Can Change The World - Haikus

I can change the world
I'll put litter in the bin
We can all do it.

I can change the world
By recycling all I can
Let's all do our bit.

I can change the world
I'll just turn off all the lights
Let's all flick that switch.

I can change the world
Be kind to other people
We should live in peace.

I can change the world
Walk to school, don't drive in cars
Help to save the world.

I can change the world
I'll share food with everyone
We'll all be the same.

Louise Kiddy (8)
Bromham CE Lower School, Bedford

Save The World

Save the world, don't be lazy
Don't drive a car to a shop nearby
Walk or ride your bike instead.
Save the world, plant lots of trees, they give you oxygen
Some plants you can eat for your tea.
Save the world, do recycle,
Don't throw everything in the bin
You can recycle lots of things like cans, plastic bottles
And lots of other things.

Hannah Cornwell (8)
Bromham CE Lower School, Bedford

Extinct

It's so sad to live
On the Earth at this time
When so many people
Put lives on the line.
Not human lives,
But animals, you see
Not everyone feels
Like you and me.
We don't want to kill
Just for the thrill
Or watch them bleed
For our needs.
So let's fight
For their right
To live on the Earth
And show us their worth.
Red panda,
Bengal tiger
Orang-utan
To name but a few
What, oh what can we do?

Megan Clayton (8)
Bromham CE Lower School, Bedford

Recycle, Recycle

Recycle, recycle, it isn't hard,
Recycle, recycle, it will save the world,
Recycle, recycle, do it to your paper,
Recycle, recycle, do it your way,
Recycle, recycle, put the cans in the special bins,
Join in the fun and recycle.

Jack Tilling (8)
Bromham CE Lower School, Bedford

Untitled

Recycle for the world
It will be good
So you should
Don't put it in the bin
Put it in the recycling tin.

Don't chuck it on the floor
Recycle even more than before
You can recycle plastic bags
Keep them for next time and save our trees
Recycle!

Taylor Bland (9)
Bromham CE Lower School, Bedford

Save The World

Save the world
What's it done wrong?
Save the world
Recycle more
Save the world
Keep it clean
Now you know what to do
Let's get down to it
I'll help too!

Charles Pope (9)
Bromham CE Lower School, Bedford

Recycle

We must recycle to save the world
To save the boys and save the girls
Please recycle, please we say
Then we'll be alive another day
If we recycle I'll shout, 'Yaay!'

Lauren Tolmie (8)
Bromham CE Lower School, Bedford

Recycle

R ecycle now to help save the planet and the environment
E verything you can mostly recycle, so do it now
C ut down on carrier bags
Y ou can help save the trees so don't waste paper, recycle now
C ut down on paper, you don't have to waste paper, you can recycle now
L et us use the things you don't want, don't keep taking things you can recycle to landfill sites
E verything you don't want to recycle goes to the landfill sites, so recycle now.

Kristie Prew (9)
Bromham CE Lower School, Bedford

Recycling

Recycle, recycle, don't throw it in the bins,
Recycle, recycle, reuse all your tins.
Recycle, recycle, do it all the time,
Recycle, recycle, don't cause any crime.
Recycling is great,
Remember to tell your mates.

Jamie Banghard (9)
Bromham CE Lower School, Bedford

Recycling

If there is rubbish on the floor that can be useful
Then pick it up and give it a tug or a pull.
Help, help, please help the world
By recycling some glasses or recycling a bulb.
Now the recycling is done we can all go home
And no one will be picking up rubbish alone.

Natasha Smiljanic (8)
Bromham CE Lower School, Bedford

Save The Planet

Save the planet, remember global warming, the planet could die
                                        if it gets too hot.
Every day when children go to school don't take the car, walk, it's cool.
Don't be in shame and full of disgrace because it's never too late
                                      to make the world a better place.
Save the animals too because they're still fresh and want to live life
                                              to the full.
You know you can save it, just try and help the planet not to die.
Be greener and don't be meaner, save the planet.

Selena Quambusch (9)
Bromham CE Lower School, Bedford

Polar Bears

Polar bears, polar bears, they are part of nature.
Polar bears, polar bears, they are dying.
Polar bears, polar bears, their environment is disappearing.
Polar bears, polar bears, they are falling in the sea.
Polar bears, polar bears, their land will soon vanish.
Polar bears, polar bears, they will probably be made extinct
If we don't do something they *will* be gone.
Polar bears, polar bears, we need you to help,
Save us *please!*

Conna Lenihan (9)
Bromham CE Lower School, Bedford

Stop The War

War, war, stop the war,
I'm sick and tired of the war continuing and people dying
So do something about it, stop the war!
It is horrible hearing people dying every day
People think war is good but it is very bad.

Tommy Hardwick (9)
Bromham CE Lower School, Bedford

Animals

A nimals are dying so please, please, please help!
N ow elephants and tigers are dying so please, please, please help!
I 'm sure they're endangered so please, please, please help!
M ammals and creatures are living things so please, please, please help!
A nimals are dying so please, please, please help!
L andfill is for animals so please, please, please help!
S houldn't cut down trees, so please, please, please help before it's too late!

Chiara Demichele (8)
Bromham CE Lower School, Bedford

Recycling

Help, help, we need an orange sack
Get an orange sack and recycle your bicycle
The world is failing and we need some help
People are littering so why don't you put your waste in an orange sack?
So come along and join our big green recycling thing
Litterbugs no, no, no, if you see something, pick it up and go, go, go!
Take it to a big green bin, don't be in disgrace, make our world
                                             a better place.

Harry Gray (8)
Bromham CE Lower School, Bedford

Nature

Nature, nature is being killed
Nature, nature has big bills
Nature, nature is really dying
Nature, nature is not smiling
Nature, nature helps us breathe
Nature, nature has lots of leaves.

Danesh Sundar (9)
Bromham CE Lower School, Bedford

Animals Of Extinction

Chimpanzees and their homes in trees
Please, please, please don't squash the bees.
Don't chuck your bags anywhere
Stop it now, do you dare.
Don't kill spiders, make them your friends
And also put fences around your hens
Or foxes, foxes, they will get them
Because they watch in their den.
And what have these animals done to you?
That is the end of my extinction poem
I hope you enjoyed it, now I'm going.

Samuel Tredray (9)
Bromham CE Lower School, Bedford

Litter

Litter, litter must go in the bin
Paper, food, chewing gum and tins
Keep our streets tidy
Bins are collected on a Friday
Fill the bins not the streets
Litterbugs we will beat.

Kayley-Ann Freame (8)
Bromham CE Lower School, Bedford

Animals In Extinction

Animals in extinction
Tigers are dying because poachers and hunters are killing them.
There are only two-thousand left in the wild because they are
                                                    dying rapidly,
So please don't kill them, help them, please help them.

Ethan Green (7)
Bromham CE Lower School, Bedford

Save The Environment

Save the environment, be eco-friendly
Walk to school or ride your bike,
Use the bins or dustbins too
Slim the bin, it's good for you.
Stop pollution, smoking, war
And try and recycle orange peel and apple core.
Recycle the cans you see on the floor,
The Coke bottles, the beer bottles, everything and more.
I love you my world, my Earth, my planet,
But soon you'll be gone if people keep treating you this way
So save the environment today!

Alex Taylor (8)
Bromham CE Lower School, Bedford

Litter

Litterbugs, litterbugs
I don't like litterbugs
If I saw you drop your litter in the river
I would shout, 'Pick it up!'
Litterbugs, litterbugs,
I don't like litterbugs
If I saw you put your litter in the bin
I would shout, 'Yippee!'

Dan Franklin (8)
Bromham CE Lower School, Bedford

Animals And Extinction

Elephants and white rhinos are close to extinction
Cutting down the rainforest means animals are losing their homes
Gorillas and orang-utans are dying in forest fires
Help before it is too late!

Emily Stanton (8)
Bromham CE Lower School, Bedford

World Of Litter

Litter is bitter,
Green is clean,
Put your rubbish in the bin.
Keep the world on a green theme.
Maybe, maybe if we do, the golden thread will pull us through!
If we try the world won't die, clean up litter to help the world.
Seeing all that gas in the air makes us feel despair.
Just a little tiny thing can make a big difference.
Run around, pick up rubbish on the ground,
Recycle, recycle that's the thing to do, maybe you can do it too!

Laura Dwyer (8)
Bromham CE Lower School, Bedford

Animals And Extinction

I love elephants, they are big and grey
But then the evil men take their tusks away.
They sell them for money
And leave their babies with no mummy.
Nature being taken away is making us sad
The people that are doing this are very bad.
The people that kill
We must make sure the patrol stations are filled.

Ellis Bell (8)
Bromham CE Lower School, Bedford

War

Why do people fight?
What gives them the right?
Soldiers fighting against each other
Using guns and aeroplanes to drop the bombs on us.

Silas Atherton (8)
Bromham CE Lower School, Bedford

It's Your World Too!

People of the world you think it's very big
But down here in the rainforest we're getting hit
Bulldozers are here knocking down our trees
Our animals are disappearing
Our climate is changing
You've ignored our plight
We haven't got much time
We need your help
The ozone does too
So come and help
It's your world too!

Katie Davis (8)
Bromham CE Lower School, Bedford

Litterbug

Litter, litter, all so bitter
Green, green, that's my theme
Keep the world nice and clean
Recycle, recycle, that's my plan
We can do it, yes we can.
Maybe, maybe, if we try
The world will never ever die!

Jessica Rowlett (8)
Bromham CE Lower School, Bedford

Litter

Look at litter, pick it up
Then all day you'll have good luck.
Then recycle all you can
Then every Friday wave to the litter man.
Recycle now!

Eloise Peacock (7)
Bromham CE Lower School, Bedford

Nature

Nature, nature beautiful and pretty,
Nature, nature unusual and colourful.
Nature, nature peaceful and natural,
Nature, nature scented and delightful.

Flowers, flowers give us oxygen,
Flowers, flowers in all sizes.
Flowers, flowers big and small,
Flowers, flowers sharp and blunt.

Trees, trees leaves fall off them,
Trees, trees old and young.
Trees, trees tall and short,
Trees, trees live in fields.

Plants, plants suck up carbon dioxide,
Plants, plants give us air.
Plants, plants all shapes and sizes,
Plants, plants have lots of parts.

Sonia Sundar (7)
Bromham CE Lower School, Bedford

Litter Is Very Bitter

When I think about global warming I feel sad
So I think I should tell you about it
Pollution makes me angry
The polar bears think it's bad
Because their homes are melting
I want to do something to stop it
I will always try to eat my food on my plate
And if I see litter I will pick it up
I hope this helps and puts things straight
I really want to save the world, yes I do
I promise I will try to save, only if you promise too!

Dani May Shaw (8)
Bromham CE Lower School, Bedford

Being Homeless

When I see a homeless person I feel very sad
And sometimes I think their life is very, very bad.
We could help them by bringing them some clothes
Or bringing them some yummy food, so they're not in a mood
Maybe take them somewhere to clean or maybe in the summer
give them sunscreen
Or give them some new shoes, some don't want help, they refuse.
I bet they wish they had a better, richer life and I bet they wish
they had a wife
I would give them some money so they could buy themselves
some honey.
Maybe in the winter we could bring them jumpers, scarves and gloves
That might make them a better life.

Gemma Ware (8)
Bromham CE Lower School, Bedford

Life As A Coke Can

Here I stand with all my family and friends, happy in the cold
cool fridge
When a big boy comes with his shiny fifty pence and takes me out
of my fridge, my home.
Then here I am alone on the cold damp grass, frightened
and very sad and lonely,
How I miss my fridge, my home.
A kick in the head, I roll across the playground where a nice girl
called Kirsty picks me up.
I wonder where I'm going, is it to a new fridge, my new home?
Oh no, it's the recycling centre, am I to be crushed?
Oh no, oh no but wait . . . no! Life is not too bad
Because I'm a new pretty key ring, my new home!

Kirsty Krzywopulski (9)
Bromham CE Lower School, Bedford

Save The Earth

We must all recycle and try not to pollute
If we don't recycle, humans will get the boot.
We must protect our planet; it's the only one we've got,
If we don't protect the ozone layer, it will get very, very hot.
We must all try to save energy and then we can live as happy
                                                                                           as can be.
I don't take my dad's car because my school's not that far
I'm gonna try to save the Earth, I'll try and try for all I'm worth.
Save the Earth!

Molly McCarthy (8)
Bromham CE Lower School, Bedford

Energy

Please stop using your cars, it's ruining the environment.
If you can just turn your lights off it can make a difference to the world.
Please don't use your car just to go to a shop down the road -
Please walk or else we could all be dead.
The sun might just pass if you don't take action now.
If you say tough and had enough you could be dead.
Don't just talk about it, do something to save our world! Please.

Madeline O'Neill (8)
Bromham CE Lower School, Bedford

Leave Nature Green

Being green is less mean to the planet we live on
So don't litter the land and kill all the plants
To help plants live it's a good idea to
Reduce, reuse and recycle
Bottles and cans, use your hands
Put them in the special bins
If we try the world won't die.

Adam Cook (8)
Bromham CE Lower School, Bedford

Make The World A Better Place

You can help the world by running, buy a bin
And pop your litter in
And that's your bit done.

Help the homeless by raising money and send it away
Maybe even give some clothes away
And they will say hooray!
Don't put cans, bottles or things like that in a bin
Put them in a recycling bag otherwise you'll make the world
a bad place.
Don't cut down rainforests you'll hurt the nature really badly,
Leave it as it is, it will be a better place!
Like all the people in the world otherwise it's very unkind.

Ellie Adams (7)
Bromham CE Lower School, Bedford

Animals And Extinction

Men wait till dusk to kill elephants for their tusks
Polar bears and tigers too, what is this world coming to?
These men think we want their fur but tell them no and make a stir!
It makes me angry, it makes me sad to think these men could
be so bad.

Lauryn Peart (8)
Bromham CE Lower School, Bedford

Polar Bears

Polar bears are white and furry
If it is hot the polar bears will die
They live in very icy places and they eat fish and seals,
they're tasty meals.

Jacob Cientanni (8)
Bromham CE Lower School, Bedford

The Golden Frogs

In the rainforest it is big
In the rainforest I knew
There was a golden frog I knew
A big, big golden frog I knew.
I thought the golden frog was good but he threw me out of the forest
for good.
There are only four remaining frogs because there's not enough
water for them to live
So help them, help them to live because it's time you took care
of them.

Scarlett Ash-Ingley (8)
Bromham CE Lower School, Bedford

Recycling

Plastic things, old tins, recycle, recycle, recycle!
Milk bottles, toilet rolls, recycle, recycle, recycle!
Garden waste, toothpaste, recycle, recycle, recycle!
Old clothes and socks with no toes, recycle, recycle, recycle!
Scrap paper, newspaper, recycle, recycle, recycle!
Plastic fantastic, what uses we can make.

Isabel Filby (7)
Bromham CE Lower School, Bedford

World War II

I saw the planes flying through the air, I heard the plane in the air
I have had basically nothing to do, someone stop this madness!
I am so worried about my father because he's a soldier
Please someone, save Great Britain.
Anyway, I never have anything to do and it's all Germany's fault.

George Kelly (8)
Bromham CE Lower School, Bedford

Litter, Litter

Litter, litter everywhere
People drop it and don't care
They should pick it up, one by one
With their friends and their mum.

It makes a mess for you and me
It makes a smell and looks ugly
It's not good and it's not clever
So let's pick it up all together

Let's learn by this and start anew
Let's go green, it's up to you.
Invite your friends, one, two, three
Let's start from now, the whole country.
It's *your* choice.

Eleanor-Rose Bown (8)
Bromham CE Lower School, Bedford

The World

The world is in danger
People are in danger
We need to stop danger
The danger is going
We need it to keep going
The danger is nearly gone
The litter is gone
But there is a new danger,
Global warming, oh no!
Now we are going to help this
Turn the heating down
Turn the temperature off
The world is getting better
The world is scared.

Jake Webster (8)
Bromham CE Lower School, Bedford

Recycle

Recycle, recycle
It's a really great thing to do
We're saving the planet
For you, you and you!
If you do not recycle
There will be a disaster
And homes will be destroyed
And the Earth will crumble
So please recycle.

Joshua Spencer (8)
Bromham CE Lower School, Bedford

Litter

Litter is bitter
Green is clean
Help the world to clean up
Please, please, please!
It is so good for you
You will be so happy when you do it
It will make you a star
So help the UK today.

Mason Ludovico (8)
Bromham CE Lower School, Bedford

Litter

Litter is bitter
Green is clean
Help the world to clean up
Please, please, please help clean up
Pick up your rubbish because the animals *will* die.

Lauren Butterworth (8)
Bromham CE Lower School, Bedford

Save The Animals

G lobal warming is bad for them
L ook after them and it will not happen
O pen your heart
B ike to school
A fter they go we have lost them
L ove them

W e may lose them
A fter they go we can't find them again
R ead and learn
M ake them happy
I would be sad to see them go
N ever disagree with them
G o to the shops on your bike to help them.

Holly Fisher (7)
Bromham CE Lower School, Bedford

The Rainforest

Bugs and beetles in their homes
Parrots in their treetop domes
Iguanas blending in
People in a house of tin
Monkeys swinging around
Waiting for a sound
The rainforest

Don't slice trees
Disturb the bees
Care for nature
Save it for later
Here's a warning
Global warming!

Joshua Gibson (8)
Bromham CE Lower School, Bedford

Climate Change

Summer
Summer, oh summer is a warm and relaxing time for holidays

Winter
Winter, oh winter is cold, freezing and rainy and snowy

Spring
Spring, oh spring is a mixture, a mixture of warm and cold.

Autumn
Autumn, oh autumn is mostly cold but has some warmth in it too.

If you want these seasons to enjoy you must look after the world.

Joshua Hands (7)
Bromham CE Lower School, Bedford

Recycling

I help to recycle at school
I help to recycle at home
I cycle to school to help the environment
Rainforests need more help
So please help!

Animals are dying and some are already extinct
So please do your bit, I've already done mine
I remind my mum to reuse carrier bags to help our planet
I sponsor a child from India, so why don't you?

Sophie Latoo (8)
Bromham CE Lower School, Bedford

Litter And Recycling

Don't be a litterbug it will make you look like a thug
Recycle our rubbish don't drop it on the floor
Put it in the bin to recycle for evermore.

George Morris (8)
Bromham CE Lower School, Bedford

Animals

Climate change is killing polar bears.
People cutting rainforests down is killing off all kinds of animals
Like gorillas, monkeys, snakes and pandas.
People who fish with hooks sometimes catch turtles.
Plastic bags suffocate birds and seals.
People not recycling or reusing are over-filling the landfill sites
                                            which pollutes the Earth.
People in Africa don't have electricity or food and some
                                            don't have homes.

Toby Haggerwood (8)
Bromham CE Lower School, Bedford

Making The World A Better Place

Recycling, the landfill is overflowing, start recycling now!
Use green and orange bins, recycling protects nature, the ozone
                                            and us.
Keep trees, protect habitats, don't cut trees down for houses or paper.
Animals, care for them, stop hunting them, if we keep hunting
                                            they're going to be extinct!
Appreciate nature, enjoy nature, take time out to look at nature.
Be friends not enemies, respect others and their beliefs, love not hate,
Stop war!

Beau Rodd (8)
Bromham CE Lower School, Bedford

Recycling

Recycled paper comes back as newspaper
Recycled newspaper comes back as toilet roll
Recycling nothing comes back as nothing
Recycle the whole world.

Joshua White (8)
Bromham CE Lower School, Bedford

The Environment

Waste food and garden clippings make compost
Recycle and compost people
Recycle or Earth, the world, gets it!
Turn your lights off
Dump the car, walk instead
Don't be a pest and don't leave your mess
Don't be a pest, clean up your mess
Grow your own veg
Keep chickens because they lay eggs and no fuel is used
Chickens are great, chickens are fun, they lay eggs from their bums!

Oliver Litchfield (8)
Bromham CE Lower School, Bedford

Where Will Polar Bears Live?

Summers are getting colder, winters are getting warmer
                                        and that cannot be right
The polar ice is melting and that's where polar bears live
So let's stop using too much electricity before polar bears vanish
                                                      out of sight
You never know it just might happen!

Sam Perkins (8)
Bromham CE Lower School, Bedford

Charity Football For Poor People

We as a nation could do more, maybe a game of charity football
People that are poor sleep on the floor
I'm glad it's not me!
Fact, poor people use cabbages for footballs, *wow!*
What a waste of food!

Kieran White (8)
Bromham CE Lower School, Bedford

Saving The World

Recycle your rubbish in the bin
Otherwise it will become the world's biggest sin.
The animals, all they want is peace
And extinction's not what we need.
We need the wars to stop
Otherwise the world will rot.
All the cars spread pollution
Oh please, oh please, what is the solution?
Make everybody have my attention
And stop the cars spreading pollution.

Jack Wheatley (8)
Bromham CE Lower School, Bedford

Recycling

Cardboard, newspaper, bottles and tins
Put them in the recycling bin.
Make them into something new,
Recycling is good to do.
Compost your old fruit and veg
And the cuttings from your hedge.
Finish your drink and crush your can
Recycling is fun to do
Don't put things that you can recycle in the rubbish bin.

Emily Fleming (8)
Bromham CE Lower School, Bedford

Recycle

Recycle, recycle, recycle today
Don't just throw your rubbish away.
Put it to use, put it to good,
Help the environment in your neighbourhood.

Charie Hislop (8)
Bromham CE Lower School, Bedford

My World

I feel angry when . . .
People are dying because people don't care
People are not equal
People are killing animals, elephants, whales and dolphins
People are hurting the environment, picking plants and wasting things.

I feel sad when. . .
Nature is being angry through cyclones and earthquakes
Forests are being chopped down
People are dropping litter and ruining the world.

I feel happy when . . .
I see things grow
People are trying to help other people who are hurt
People are passing laws that stop people doing bad things.

Sophie Nixon (8)
Bromham CE Lower School, Bedford

Recycling

Recycle round the world; it makes a better place,
I put my litter in the bin; it makes a lot of space.
I put my bottles in the orange sack,
They get taken away and come back.
I give my toys to charity they go to someone new
So they have something new to do.

Skye Haggith (7)
Bromham CE Lower School, Bedford

Recycle

Recycle, recycle, it's a good thing to do
The one and only person that is recycling is you!
Recycle cans, paper and tins,
Please, please, please don't use the bins!

Rachel Fish (8)
Bromham CE Lower School, Bedford

The War

I could see the soldiers marching up and down by the old inn door.
I could hear the last zap of the pylons.
I could feel the dust on the tanks.
I could taste the tears as they ran down my face, I felt sad.
I could smell the dust in the wind blowing.
Everyone in the old inn was trying to bail out, but the guns started
                                           and people were trapped.
It was too late and I could not save them, I got myself out as quick
                                                     as I could.

Dalziel Holder (9)
Dallow Primary School, Luton

Climate Changes

Floods are very scary and lots of people die
The climate changes and it is not nice
Storms cut the electricity and there is no power
Tornadoes are super strong winds that blow away the houses
Tsunamis are powerful waves that smash to the ground and people die
There are lots of climates, some are strong and some are
                                           just the seasons.

Daniel Fedorov (9)
Dallow Primary School, Luton

The War

I could see the soldiers marching up and down by the old inn door.
I could hear the last zap of the pylon.
I could feel the dust on the tanks.
It was so sad, it was time for war now and houses were being
                                               bombed by grenades,
That's what I could taste.
I could smell people's blood dripping.

Mohammed Humza Raja (10)
Dallow Primary School, Luton

Air Pollution

Smoke is racing spirits, making progress on spreading cancer.
Smoke is murderous fire, polluting, encircling the precious Earth.
Smoke is like a dog, overcast like a murderous shadow.
Smoke is a cautious trap, brainwashing you carefully,
You can see the fifty feet building being covered with venomous
                                            gas or smoke,
As you smell the incredible nasty smoke you hear the pollution
                                            whizzing past your air,
Incredible feeling of invasion, do something about it hero!

Hamad Jamil (9)
Dallow Primary School, Luton

Racism

R osa Parks went to jail for not giving her seat to a white person
A lso there is still racism in many countries
C alling people racist names or making fun of their religion is racism
I personally believe that racism is really horrible
S ome think it is great fun
M ake sure you don't do it.

Ameena Hussain (11)
Dallow Primary School, Luton

Clean It Up!

Clean it up so the litter will be brushed away.
Clean it up so we can see the difference between blue and green.
Clean it up so the blue and green will shine in our eyes.
Clean it up so we don't see any litter any time, any day.
Clean it up so we can live in a world of greenness,
Clean it up!

Halimah Isbag (11)
Dallow Primary School, Luton

War

War is a problem, war is a calamity,
All the soldiers are tolerating the pain
I will one day make all the soldiers sign a contract then I will
                                            accomplish my destiny.

War is a problem, war is a calamity,
If you were there you would see what happens and you would
                                                feel sorrow.
I can taste the mutinous smoke of the guns drifting into my nostrils.
I can finally smell the fresh blood dripping onto the ground.
I can hear the dreadful screaming from a young soldier's mouth.

War is a problem, war is a calamity
When will the war ever stop?

Monwara Bibi (9)
Dallow Primary School, Luton

War And Poverty

I can see an enormous group of cold, starving, hopeless children.
I can also see a fierce, awful and gigantic war or battle.
I can hear gunshots killing an innocent child.
I feel children holding my shirt begging for food and money.
I taste dust rushing into my mouth as if it's the spirit of the boy
                                             begging for food.
I smell the blood of the soldiers.

Abid Ahmed & Samiun Rahman (10)
Dallow Primary School, Luton

War

War is wine dripping from bodies.
War is the creation of blood, Heaven or Hell, it's your choice.
Formidable Hell gaining closer and closer,
War is waiting with its teeth, sucking up all of the life.

Shakil Ahmed & Abu-Sayeed Miah (10)
Dallow Primary School, Luton

Environment Problems

As soon as I walked into the countryside,
I saw the grass with trash on it like a junkyard.
All I could smell was the dreadful scent of garbage,
Everything I touched was polluted with junk.
The birds screeching to death with all the pollution was all I heard.
I feel the people should chuck their litter in the bins
And help the environment!
Do you have the intelligence to do that?

Rohima Nessa & Anisa Khan (10)
Dallow Primary School, Luton

Small Changes

You can walk far because it's better than a car.
Kick start your day the healthy way,
Put your rubbish in the bin
You can flatten cardboard so it's thin
Just remember before you throw
Into which bin your rubbish should go.
A few small changes, that's all it will take
To make our world a better place.

Neve Gordon-Farleigh (8)
Elm Road Primary School, Wisbech

Could We Save Our World?

Our world, our world
We all live in it though
How could we save it?
Recycle it of course!
Brown bin, blue bin and green bin
Tins, paper and vegetable peel, they will all go in the bin
After you finish with it please recycle it properly
Then this will help make our world a better place to be.
Remember, save our world from litter.

Grace Cherry (8)
Elm Road Primary School, Wisbech

Being Green

Do your best, try to be green
Think of the planet, healthy and clean.
This is a solution for less pollution
Switching off a light is a little thing
But it could save the world we're living in.
Throwing your litter in a careless way
Could lead to rats, filth and decay.
Recycling is an important part for giving the world a healthy heart.
So do your best, try to be green
For the planet and all that is on it to stay healthy, strong and clean.

Mia Churchill (8)
Elm Road Primary School, Wisbech

What Other People Are Doing

When you've just got up in the morning and you want to chase a bee
Other people are cutting down loads of trees.
When it's your breakfast and you've broken your thumb
Someone just lost his arm while using a gun!
When it's lunch and you're meant to be learning brass
Other people are making pollution by using their cars.
When it's teatime and you're waiting for your nice meat
Someone is trying to sleep on a main street.
But then you wake up and it has all been a dream . . . or has it?

Niamh Murdoch (9)
Holmer Green Junior School, Holmer Green

War

I signed up to be a soldier but now I regret it.
I jump into the field, hand firmly tight against the trigger, *fire!*
I feel like I'm serving England well so I penetrate the main battle,
I see one of our men fall to the ground, not dead but wounded,
                                                    I haul him to shelter.
Silence, I look over to see we've won the battle, *hooray!*

Jacob Pompe (9)
Holmer Green Junior School, Holmer Green

Don't Drop, Just Stop

Littering,
A sin,
Not putting your remains in the bin.

It's bad,
It's sad,
It never makes us glad.

Don't drop,
Just stop,
Or you will be caught by the cop.

The litter in the sea makes us spit out our tea
The pollution in the sky really makes us cry
And the rubbish on land makes the Earth feel bland.

So please now halt
And realise your fault.
Save the Earth,
Don't litter,
Don't drop, *just stop.*

Jamie Brazier (10)
Holmer Green Junior School, Holmer Green

Anti-Drugs Poem

One thing that's clogging up the world
Is the drugs that people are taking.
They muck up your brain, will drive you insane
This must be something we can stop.
The cannabis, the heroin,
It all drives me mad.
The cocaine, the steroids,
This cannot go on.

So many drug dealers,
Don't they know what they're doing?
If you're against drugs and you want your say
Then you are doing the right thing.

Robert Huw Bagley (11)
Holmer Green Junior School, Holmer Green

A Poem To Change The World

When I'm older what I want to see,
are the polar bears or the bumblebees.
I mentioned this because it's sad
that killing animals is really bad
for medicine, fur, clothes and meat
even for the shoes on my feet.

Moving this thing on as I carry out my song,
I'll start on pollution, now *that's* wrong.
Driving around in your car,
when you're not even that far.
The time has come - we need to talk
all I ask - just get up and walk!

I can't name all these things, it would take forever
don't do these things, never, *never!*
Don't do it or I'll go crazy,
come on . . . don't be lazy!

Hannah May Leonard (10)
Holmer Green Junior School, Holmer Green

CO_2!

CO_2, CO_2
Cars is one
They let out smoke
And there are too many.

Lights, lights, on all night.
It's like Las Vegas
Turn off the lights
And let the sunlight in.

Power plants, power plants
Too much smoke
I cover my mouth to stop my cough.

Vicki Tutt (10)
Holmer Green Junior School, Holmer Green

Litter, Litter!

Litter, litter
Thrown around
Messier, messier
By the pound.
Litter, litter
On the table, on the chair.
Litter, litter
On the street
It's even stuck to my feet!
Litter is here,
Litter is there,
Litter is dangled in my hair.
I am annoyed,
I am stressed,
I just want a big rest.

Fiona Hollings (11)
Holmer Green Junior School, Holmer Green

War

War is terrible
Don't let those guns begin,
War is disgraceful
Men go hungry and start to get thin.
War is excruciating
Blood draining from skin,
War is horrific
It causes death to your kin.
War is hopeless
Starting war is a sin,
War is horrendous
Put war in the bin!

Shaun Jillians (9)
Holmer Green Junior School, Holmer Green

War And Terrorism

I see no wisdom in their eyes,
I see no courage, I feel those tears
They strike again.

These people are forced to stop
Forced to stop and end
The people devastate
They make some lives a threat.

They don't agree, they don't make sense
Henceforth they don't regret
Agreement is a key to life.
So please, I shout out loud
Stop fighting in a crowd
Or if you're solo you cause a row.
Please, I beg and plead
You know this is not a need
Stop war,
Stop terrorism,
Stop fear,
Stop!

Cameron Garden (11)
Holmer Green Junior School, Holmer Green

Anti-Vandalism

Vandalism, it's against the law
Everything ruined, that's all you ever saw.
Walls covered in graffiti mess
It makes you sad, it makes you stressed.
Clocks strike twelve, they start to appear
You have nothing to do except stay clear.
Smashed windows, broken doors,
It's almost like new city wars.
This needs to stop, it is no good
Vandalism, can't you see it should?

Emma Cooper (10)
Holmer Green Junior School, Holmer Green

Pollution

Pollution is killing us
Just as well as the world,
We try to fight
But it bounces back.
There is one thing that we can do
To make the world a better place
Take the bus, take the train,
Share with your neighbours
Just don't hurt the world again.
I'm getting angry,
I'm getting annoyed,
People just listen
Our world is being destroyed!

Catherine Kirby (11)
Holmer Green Junior School, Holmer Green

Poem About Vandalism

Our world, big and beautiful
But with this horrible vandalism
This big place is looking rundown.
With graffiti, glass smashing
And all the other factors
Our world is now a dump
Scattered down the dark alleys
On bus stops, on houses all around.
Drunk people drink and drive,
Smashing bottles, breaking cars,
But if we can stop this behaviour
This world will be a better place.

Mason Wright (11)
Holmer Green Junior School, Holmer Green

My World

I made myself a world
My core,
My crust,
My boiling hot lava,
My rocks colliding together.

I created myself some land
My water,
My air,
My soil,
My grass bright green,
My sea a gentle blue,
My plants in amazing colours.

I formed myself the weather
My sun,
My wind,
My rain dropping water,
My snow freezing cold,
My hail hard as stones.

I added myself the creatures
My mammals,
My reptiles,
My humans unique in every way.

What a shame my humans changed it all,
My world is polluted by the cars and others,
You could make a difference, save your world.

Verity Hunn (9)
Maltman's Green School, Gerrards Cross

How To Save The World

You can recycle paper and things that are recyclable,
You can reuse things that are reusable.
You can reduce things that can be reduced
So get up and help save the world.

Pippa Nester (8)
Maltman's Green School, Gerrards Cross

I Like My Planet Nice And Clean

I like my planet nice and clean
But you can tell where mankind's been.
We have made so much pollution
We must find a new solution.
We must do something quite drastic
To rid the Earth of so much plastic.
Always pick up all your litter
And perhaps the world will start to glitter.
If all the countries stopped their fight
We may find the future's bright.
If we stopped cutting down the trees
There'd be more room for birds and bees.
We need to build more people houses
So they've a place to hang their trousers.
We have to save tigers and pandas
But it depends on what mankind does.
So if you want a world serene
You should think of going green!

Jenna Arnot (7)
Maltman's Green School, Gerrards Cross

Recycling Is Cool

Me and you together
Can make the world better,
By being nice and kind
To everything around.
We only have one planet
And we all need to man it,
So whoever you are
Or whatever you do,
Get in the groove
Recycling is cool.

Ellie Green (8)
Maltman's Green School, Gerrards Cross

Animal Picnic

There is a night
That every year
The mayors of the animals gather here.

The night is tonight
And they all gather to
Discuss all the things that animals do.

Before they come to the annual picnic
Invitations are sent to the mole and the greedy tick,
To the seal and the flea that travels with the cat,
To the worm, to the parrot and to the mayor of all rats.

There is only one species which is *never* invited
For the human being is sure to cause bloodshed.
Only last year, to our great surprise,
The Cuban Kite, we did not see, flying through the skies
'They're extinct, they're extinct,' we heard faded cries
From the mayor of the goldfish inside
His new goldfish bowl made from pure gold and painted with blue dragonflies.

The goldfish was right
The Cuban Kites were extinct.
'But how?' I hear you shout.
It's those human beings
Destroying the world and turning it inside out!

Victoria Taylor (11)
Maltman's Green School, Gerrards Cross

There Is A Solution To Pollution

Don't just throw your rubbish on the ground
Cycle to school and work and all around.
Recycling is a really good thing to do
Glass, paper and food waste too.
All these things will help the world to be
A better place for you and me.

Milly Trenwith (8)
Maltman's Green School, Gerrards Cross

Make My World A Better Place

Think green
Think clean
Let's start with litter
It makes me feel bitter.
It pollutes the air
And gets stuck in animals' hair.
So recycle, reuse,
And start to enthuse.
There's poverty about the world
And around the Earth, death is curled.
People are homeless and have diseases
Yet no one listens or answers their pleas.
The climate is changing
The sun is blazing.
Litter created global warming
Now towards our Earth the sun is swarming.
Animals are dying, dead, extinct
So have a moment and just rethink.
There are too many wars
With no reasonable cause.
So hands up if you care
There's no time to spare.
Let's make our world a better place.

Rebecca Sillett (10)
Maltman's Green School, Gerrards Cross

Saving The Planet

We love our planet; we should all be looking after it
Animals are dying and losing their homes
People are cutting down trees and forests
And don't care about animals.
They give us food and without them we will die.

Emily Lue-Fong (7)
Maltman's Green School, Gerrards Cross

Make The World A Better Place

Wars, wars, wars, please make them stop,
Be friends with everyone and love them all a lot.

Litter, litter, litter, it can kill animals,
It can kill all types of them, big and small.

Diseases, diseases, diseases, they can really kill,
Pay a little money and people won't be so ill.

Racism, racism, racism, it really, really hurts,
So don't be a meano and treat people like dirt.

Recycling, recycling, recycling, do it all the time,
The people collect it in the morning so put it out at night.

Homelessness, homelessness, homelessness, people are that
They have no bed to sleep in; they just sleep with the rats.

Psst, in a few weeks time they'll be sleeping with the fishes!

Pollution, pollution, pollution, share a car today,
Don't let the world decay away.

So be a friend
Don't let the world end!

Gagan Grewal (10)
Maltman's Green School, Gerrards Cross

How To Make The World A Better Place

To make the world a better place there's no time to waste
To keep clean the Earth it will be all the effort worth.
Let's contain all our waste paper, glass and plastic
And the results will be so fantastic!
Now, if the whole world works together
Just imagine what it will mean to soil, earth and weather.
Come let us start to recycle as of today
And help the recycling men take it all away.

Annicke Van Wyk (7)
Maltman's Green School, Gerrards Cross

Poverty

Tears fall like rain onto the dark dry ground
A black cloud hanging over Africa, death is the only sound.
It's poverty in Africa, their home is completely bare
They need food and water to live, please go and take it there.
Think of all the people who die there every day,
Let's go over there and put the sadness at bay.
Come on everybody, before it's too late
Go and help their country to relieve that terrible state.
Let's go and rebuild Africa, the government don't mind
Go and see the children, it's happiness they find.
Even in that terrible scene they still laugh and play
Even though that ground they stand on is harder than clay.
So everyone, join hand in hand
Let's go and rescue them from that terrible land.
It's everywhere, the news, some books
But no one even bothers to look.
I'm helping, what about you?
Come on, you can join in too!

Jemima Lomax (10)
Maltman's Green School, Gerrards Cross

I Wish

I wish people recycled.
I wish we could not cut down trees.
I wish we could live in harmony.
I wish animals could live as long as we do.
I wish we could share the world.
I wish we could help each other.
I just know we could make a difference to the world.

Louise Thomassin (8)
Maltman's Green School, Gerrards Cross

The Dust Is Disturbed

The dust is disturbed
As a man's foot pounds
The dusty grey ground,
The bang of a gun
A war breaks out!
They scream and shout,
The dying man writhes
On the dusty grey ground,
Only one may win.
They all commit murder
As do the people
Who kill wildlife.
So stop wars and extinction
To make the world a better place
As an animal dies
The dust is disturbed.

Charlotte Williams (10)
Maltman's Green School, Gerrards Cross

Homeless Mary

There was once a happy family
All together happy as could be,
A few weeks later there was a new joiner
She was called Mary Lee.
Now Mary was homeless
Homeless as could be,
Now everyone asked 'What's to do,
What's to do with Mary Lee?'

Eleanor Thornton (8)
Maltman's Green School, Gerrards Cross

The World

If we could stop pollution, disease and war
This dirty world would be a better place for sure.
The homeless need money for water and food
Don't forget litter; that we must include.
Litter is pollution that changes the weather
We also need to save animals and birds; each and every feather.
Rainforests are being cut down
Each will soon become a ghost town.
The oxygen we get is from trees
And if we stop cutting we will save the chimpanzees
So let us all recycle each and every day
This will make pollution slowly drift away.
Save electricity by switching off the TV
Doing all of this will make the world happy.

Sophia Scott (10)
Maltman's Green School, Gerrards Cross

Forget Cars

Forget cars, their pollution is bad,
Forget cars, maybe just a tad.
If everyone forgot about cars in the world
The sun would come out and your hair would get curled.
So start to run and walk, it's fun
Or run a race, hooray! You've won!

Annabelle Corfield (8)
Maltman's Green School, Gerrards Cross

Make My World A Better Place

Why isn't the world a better place with a brighter time ahead?
We need to wake up from our dreams and think of what's been said.

Animals' extinction, soon the wild will disappear
Save their lives from rubbish tips, the time to act is here.

Think of people with no home, no family, no friends,
No one that cares for them, bring that to an end.

Diseases all over the world that make people die,
Why are we letting this happen, why, oh tell me why?

Ice is melting into water then animals lose homes,
Don't sit at your computer screen, don't leave climate change alone.

Pollution's not just an awful thing; it's also an awful smell,
Cut down the rubbish now, oh now and lock it in a cell.

Poverty is fists and fights and hunger joined by thirst,
Give people in Africa a proper life and an extra happy burst.

Make the world a better place with a brighter time ahead,
We need to wake up for our dreams and think of what's been said!

Georgia Bingham (10)
Maltman's Green School, Gerrards Cross

Recycling

Please, please recycle
It is easy as can be
Take things like glass
And cans and recycle them.
Get your recycle box
And recycle, recycle.

Madeleine Champion (8)
Maltman's Green School, Gerrards Cross

Homeless Man

He sits there
Watching time slide like a snail
People staring at him in disappointment
Shivering while being stared at
Sworn at, spat at and called names
Isolated in time
Angry and annoyed with his life.

Rejected by the Earth
Rejected by his family and friends
Frightened by the night sky
Watching darkness fill him with sadness
And no hope of a better life
Watching himself die in time
Watching himself die inside
His friendship with the world is over.

Jibril Rashid (11)
Queen Edith Primary School, Cambridge

Homeless

The boiling hot summer
People walking past chatting to their friends
When you have no one to talk to
Lonely.

In the autumn
Covered in a bed of leaves
Wonder why no one helps you
Confused.

Freezing in the winter snow
So numb you can't feel your fingers
Scared of everyone walking past
Hunched in your sleeping bag
Neglected.

Daniel Turner (11)
Queen Edith Primary School, Cambridge

Rainforest

Big green rainforest,
In its proud version of life,
Waiting for danger to come along,
Again,
Like nights ago,
When half of it was destroyed.

Animals are rushing,
To save their children's lives,
No one can help them,
No one wants to,
No one really cares.

Will their lives get better?
Can they help themselves?
No,
Their lives are not the same,
Not like the other day.

Natalia Rogowska (11)
Queen Edith Primary School, Cambridge

The Tapir

Nimble and quick
He creeps across the forest ground
Hiding from predators
Trying not to make a sound

Protecting the young
From the panthers among
The vegetation
Which is so quickly fading

His proboscis sways in the breeze
The white-tipped ears twitch
The calf cowers at his knees
As the tree crashes down

Cruelly robbed of their habitats
The lowly tapir
Just so the trees can be made into paper.

Phoebe Wheeler (11)
Queen Edith Primary School, Cambridge

Just Yesterday

Just yesterday
I was towering over
Reaching towards the calm blue sky
I was standing tall
Wrapping in curled ivy

The soft gentle breeze passed by
Fluttering the leaves
Upon my skin
Firmly settled along my arms
The bird sung songs of colours

They sing an enchanted
Mesmerising song
I listen to the melodies
Floating in the air

I was the rainforest
Just yesterday
The sun shone through me
Its beams shining
Showing dancing people silhouetted
Across the floor

Small showers of pearl raindrops
Hung like necklaces
Around me
Settling on leaves
Shimmering

Until it ended
The parrot's scream
The only warning
A deep menacing growl
Shook into a roar

The birds fled in a desperate attempt
Terror boomed in my ears
Deafening cries
Filled the forest

Shark teeth ate through
Blood-red sap seeped out
Scared and horrified
I had stiffened up
To try to block out
The murderous terror

Now today
I lie in logs
Rain pelts on my cold hard skin
No longer pearls
But stones which beat my back

I hear birds
In the distance
Mourning their loss
By the horizon

The dreary thick air covers me
As I lie on the muddy ground
Thinking of what I had when I was a rainforest
Just yesterday
Which was stolen from me
Gone
In just one day.

Anthea Chui (11)
Queen Edith Primary School, Cambridge

From 1000 To 1

Extinction.
Yesterday,
There were thousands of us.
Now,
We are only five.
Afraid.
Afraid of you,
Humans.
It could be me or all of my family
Who knows?
We might be converted,
From an animal
Into a coat.
We may end up in a zoo
Surrounded by humans,
Cameras, flashes.
From a thousand to one.

Natalia de la Cueva (11)
Queen Edith Primary School, Cambridge

Why Me?

They torment me at school
Because of my colour
In the streets they do it too
Trampling on my feet as they barge past
Shoving me, nudging me
Hoping that a miracle will come down
From the heavens
Why me?

Crying in the corner at school
Blizzards of tears fall
From bloodshot eyes
Scrunched up in darkness
Isolated, alone
Deserted, disowned
On planet sorrow
Why me?

Holly Hayes (11)
Queen Edith Primary School, Cambridge

Refugee Camp

They stand there
Staring with eyes of despair
Staring out to the world of freedom
Never getting out,
Trapped!

Their home country was loved,
A missing friend
But now it's an old, dusty bomb site.
They were evacuated because of wars
And it is treacherous so they can't go back.

The prison guards beat them,
Spit on them
And judge their freedom by their colour.
Taken away from friends and family
Not knowing where they are,
Dead? In another country?
Never knowing
All their hard work counts for nothing.
Trapped,
Can't get out!

No one deserves to be treated this way
They have been rejected because of their colour,
Not fair.

William Sharp (11)
Queen Edith Primary School, Cambridge

Bullying

I am a bully
I push people about all day
Picking on people that are younger
Smaller

I walk about with my head up high
Waiting for people to move out of the way
I do what I want
Nobody tells me what to do

I'm selfish, strong and mighty
I'm arrogant and I know it all
I don't try to be cool, I am cool

I threaten people
Give me money
If they don't that's a
Huge
Mistake to play with

People tell me that
I should change
But I'm always going to be a
Bully.

Cristina D'Uva (11)
Queen Edith Primary School, Cambridge

Different

I am different
And proud to be
Just me, I suppose.

When I go to school
I am
Invisible
And there is a reason
Behind it all.
Because I'm different.

I sit at my uninhabited desk,
Just waiting and waiting
Till someone, someday
Shows their face.

I will hunger for friends
And to be paid attention to.
To be favoured and run after.
But it won't happen
Because I'm different.

Puja Chudasama (11)
Queen Edith Primary School, Cambridge

Homeless Man

The man snuggles up
As he lies outside,
When the people walk by and spit at him,
He hides under his sleeping bag,
He gets a kick and cries in pain.

The man sniffs around the bin for some food,
He begs for money to buy some food,
He shouts in agony as his tummy
Cries for food.

The man lies outside at night,
As he shivers
He estimates how cold it is,
He scrunches up to get body heat,
But it doesn't help.

The man tries to get up but gets shoved
Straight back down as he is
Ejected from the world.

Joseph Fallon (11)
Queen Edith Primary School, Cambridge

Racism

I walk through the school gates,
Pressed against the wall
Edging nearer to school,
Until suddenly he and his gang
Come out of nowhere.
They strike at me
With full force.

In class people come and
Ask uncomfortable questions.
I get mean-spirited notes
Left in my drawer
Waiting for me to come
And reveal them.

I cannot tell anyone
He says so.
If I do he will ruin my life.
It is already ruined
I explain to him
But he just starts calling me names
And thumps me harder.

At playtime I sit alone
Crying inside.
Sometimes I wish I was the same colour
As everyone else
This is what he is doing
Mesmerising my mind.

Out of school is even worse,
They stroll over,
Proud towards my house.
They lie to my mum,
They say they are my friends.
So she lets them in
Of course they batter
My arms and legs,
They whack my face with fists.

Rhian Hughes (11)
Queen Edith Primary School, Cambridge

Acid Rain Is A Big Pain!

Acid rain
Acid rain
Gives the plants so much pain
Dead plants
Grey plants
Looks so much like burnt plants
Down, down, down
Falls the acid rain
Power stations, cars, lorries, trucks
All pollute the sky in a big, big rush!
Hurry up, we need to save our world!

Eleanor Wager & Ellen Wallwork (8)
St Alban's Catholic Primary School, Cambridge

Acid Rain

It damages the environment
Pollution goes up in the air
It makes trees look burnt
But we don't seem to care

It hurts the Acropolis
For buildings it's such a pain
Many ancient temples
It's much to cry of shame

What is it?
It's *acid rain!*

Megan Meredith-Rodriguez (9)
St Alban's Catholic Primary School, Cambridge

Global Warming

Have you ever taken a moment
To think what you're doing to help global warming?
The ice caps are melting into the sea
As global warming looks on happily
Acid rain is moving towards the sky
When it rains the plants all die
Acid rain is the culprit for the river dolphin dying
The floods and droughts are getting silly
Have you ever thought how you are helping global warming?
It's you, it's me, it's everyone
But we can change and stop our planet dying.

Ellen Curran & Graciela (9)
St Alban's Catholic Primary School, Cambridge

Acid Rain

Acid rain brings up the pain
Acid rain, this is not a game
So listen up folks, this is not a big joke
You could ride your bike or walk and talk
And that will make a big change to our world
And gives us a big twirl. So remember
Stop acid rain!

Saskia Capetti (9)
St Alban's Catholic Primary School, Cambridge

Acid Rain

Acid rain stop falling down,
The plants are beginning to die and drown.
Acid rain is such a pain,
It's such a shame, it's acid rain,
You should stop using a car,
So you can become a big green star.
There's always a solution,
To stop the pollution,
So try to stop acid rain!

Aisling Munnelly (8)
St Alban's Catholic Primary School, Cambridge

Acid Rain

Acid rain
Is such a pain
To stop pollution
We need a solution
So get an energy light
Not too much of a fright
And it's not too insane
Or too much of a shame
So do something gold
And save the world.

Sean-Francis Calvey (9)
St Alban's Catholic Primary School, Cambridge

Poverty

People are poor,
People are sad,
Having no money is driving us mad.

People are rich,
People are happy,
Some can't afford to by their baby's nappy.

They are so lucky,
They don't understand,
Being so rich is on high demand.

Sitting at home,
Buying a car every day,
Some can't afford toys to play.

Our babies are dying
From no food or drink
You have water coming out of the sink.

Just give us some money
We just want to play
Just give us some money
It will make our day.

Pauline Mwakulegwa (11)
St Joseph's Junior School, Luton

War

War solves nothing
War kills
War is wrong

War is immature
War haunts families
War scares all

War takes lives
War steals friendship
War claims loved ones.

Daniel Staniforth (11)
St Joseph's Junior School, Luton

Poverty

People with money,
People without,
Why can't you lend some,
Without the big shout?

So help out,
Don't let your country down,
Come on and help,
Then you'll wear a crown.

It's a big problem in our town,
They need our money,
Without a big sound,
Give your money.

Homeless, poor, unhappy,
No water or no food,
It really doesn't put them,
In a good mood.

In Africa and India,
There's lots to do,
Put in a water tap
And a new loo.

Barnardos and CAFOD,
Helping them through,
People giving money,
To help do what they need to do.

People with money,
People without,
Why can't you lend some,
Without the big shout?

Emily Godfrey (11)
St Joseph's Junior School, Luton

War, War

War, war everywhere
People shooting here and there
People scared with all their fears
The loud noises hurt their ears

Snipers hiding low and high
Sitting silently watching people die
Who will win, no one knows
But when will the war close?

Bombs exploding all around
Making a horrific sound
Blood spilt every day
People's faces turning grey.

Joe Grossi & Jordan West (11)
St Joseph's Junior School, Luton

War

War, war is everywhere
Bombs are flying in the air
People are hurt
But most of you don't really care

Bombs are flying
People are dying
Soldiers are trying
Children are crying

Stop this nonsense
This is a crime
Try and help please
There's not a lot of time.

Ben Murray (11)
St Joseph's Junior School, Luton

War

Who will be left?
Hopefully me!
Or will I be gone
Like my family?

Will they take care
Or let us be?
What will be left
For them and me?

I feel scared
No one's here
Not even a mouse
Anywhere near.

No one to love me
No one to share
How do I live?
How do I bear?

I'd be better off dying
There's no point to live
What else can I do?
There's no more to give.

Jessica Gajewski (11)
St Joseph's Junior School, Luton

What Is Happening To The World?

The world is a bad place,
The war is really bad,
Racism is a horrible thing,
It makes people sad.

Animals are being tortured,
Pollution is hurting the woods,
The rainforest is dying,
Poverty needs the goods.

Thomas Mayne (11)
St Joseph's Junior School, Luton

War

War, war
is very bad,
People die
so we get sad.

Shooting, shooting
with their guns,
Now we don't have
tea and buns.

Bombs, bombs
are set off by tanks,
They may be left by
a river bank.

Soldiers are hurt
so now they're dying,
Helicopters are set off
and now they're flying.

They all at least
have fun,
But they say
it's no time for fun.

Amber Hutton (11)
St Joseph's Junior School, Luton

War Is Bad

War is bad
It has happened to my great grandad
He became shy
When he found out that he could die

War has got tanks
Which has a bomb
War has guns
They can kill one another.

Niamh Timmons McCullagh (10)
St Joseph's Junior School, Luton

Litter

Litter, litter everywhere,
We throw it there without a care,
Please stop littering, please do,
Or the government will come after you.

Litter, litter all on the ground,
We throw it there without a sound,
Soon there won't be a clear patch,
Not even for an egg to hatch.

Stop litter! Stop it now!
Even if you don't know how,
Why do people litter, why oh why?
They are just making Mother Earth cry.

Tiarnan Doherty (11)
St Joseph's Junior School, Luton

Animal Extinction

Animals are dead
because cruel people chop off their heads.
Many animals get covered with blood
or are lying dead in the mud.

Their skin is rotting day by day
because of this the killer will pay.
Flies hover in the air,
looking for a dead animal to share.

Thulani Ncube (11)
St Joseph's Junior School, Luton

Recycling

Recycling, recycling, how can we help it?
Recycling helps the world to make it a better place.

Streets are full of rubbish,
Bedrooms are full of old mouldy sweets,
So all we need around the house is recycling.

The more you recycle, the more comfort you will have.

Kinga Nawrocka (11)
St Joseph's Junior School, Luton

A Wonderful Place

When the world is a wonderful place, people have fun
And no one should throw litter.
The cotton clouds pass by me,
What a shame that kids are risking their lives in boxes
And anything they can fit in.
It really touches me inside,
I don't know why we have more money and food,
I know my guilty heart is filled with darkness.

Lien Fox
Stanton School, Milton Keynes

Ha! What A Wonderful World!

The world is a wonderful place,
With amazing wonderful and shiny water
And the beautiful birds singing beautifully
The green, fresh grass, the world is like Heaven
The world is a wonderful place
Every day, every hour, every minute, every second of the day
The world is fantastic in every way
But what a shame that people don't care.

Kirston Woods (10)
Stanton School, Milton Keynes

The Way Life Should Not Go . . .

How should it go?
Poverty takes over, war
spreads, disease comes into
place. Poverty　　moves times to
death and confusion.　But disease
can be joined. . .　　　long black
legs and its　　　　　blood-red
　　　　　　　　　　heart . . . War
　　　　　　　　　takes its part
　　　　　　　　in this as well,
　　　　　　　innocent people
　　　　　　people killed in
　　　　　　a shower of
　　　　　　pointlessness.
How did
it all start
and . . .

Why?

Christopher Arnold (11)
Stanton School, Milton Keynes

The Wicked Life

The wicked life of poverty rains overloads of poor families.
The wicked life of poverty; tearful, lonely and unsafe.
It brings death, a lack of food and normally at a young age.
It brings starvation to many people, hunger
They go without and they are under nourished.
We should do something about it because they are not
　　　　　　　　　　　　　　　　　　　　　as lucky as us.
As we have PSPs and Nintendo Wiis and even more food,
They don't have all that so that is that.

Sasha Stoker-Jackson (11)
Stanton School, Milton Keynes

Odd One Out

Different height,
Different size,
Different colour skin and eyes.

People around me
Laugh and say
You're a different colour
Go away.

I wonder what to do
Or say
I never wanted to come anyway.

I wonder what my mother will say
I never wanted her to know

The other children
Pointed and said will you go away
We don't want you to stay.

Shelby Fuller (10)
Stanton School, Milton Keynes

Racism! It's Got To Stop!

Black, white,
Brown, yellow,
Some depressed,
People feel
Like they don't belong,
It tugs at my heart strings,
Makes me sob,
It should stop,
So pull together
Figure it out,
Everyone belongs
Whether they are
Black, white,
Brown or yellow.

Rachael Wayman (10)
Stanton School, Milton Keynes

My Box

Welcome to my box
It isn't really a lot
It gets me very far
So can you drop a single penny in my pot?

I beg for money
All the time
I feel like I have done something wrong
Something like a crime.

I get scared at night
It gives me a fright
I see out of sight
A flash of light.

All by yourself, ready or not
No more tears to cry
I know this is sad to say
But you might as well die.

Courtenay Wooding (11)
Stanton School, Milton Keynes

War Is An Awful Thing

War is an awful thing
It is not like well cool bling
It makes you want to scream and shout
But when it's over it will make you sing.

You must not go outside
You must turn off the lights
If you go outside you might die
If you even see, you won't sleep tonight.

When it was over we all celebrated
But some of us cried
It was so good that the war was gone
But there were funerals for the people that died.

Lisa Ann Waite (11)
Stanton School, Milton Keynes

No More Help!

Mum's died of malaria
Dad died which is scarier
Living with my little brother
He keeps asking for my mother

Growing weary, going thin
Malnutrition's kicking in
Out on the side, all alone
My brother by my side wishing for a home

Living in a dump, acting like a grump
Toxic fumes in the air
Residents just don't really care.

My brother's ill, I start to yelp
I'm crying now, got *no more help!*

Rachel Dosunmu (11)
Stanton School, Milton Keynes

The No Resolution For Pollution!

There's air and water pollution,
Smoky, hot or cold,
There is no resolution,
You're tired of being old.

You're making global warming,
It is not good for us,
You drive cars and vans,
Stop making such a fuss!

Gases, petrol and toxics,
Can cause climate change,
They're very bad for people,
They come in a different range.

Cara Brooker (11)
Stanton School, Milton Keynes

Is It Over Yet?

Is it over yet?
Not another war,
Countries fighting about the law,
The devastation of our nation,
Men are fighting,
Will they ever start reuniting?

Not another war,
Off goes the siren, time to hide,
Guns start firing, Mum by my side,
The massacre goes on, everything is crazy,
Has the world gone wrong?

Not another war,
The air is empty,
No more gunfire,
No more bangs,
No more bombs,
Is it over now?

Iman Mohammed (10)
Stanton School, Milton Keynes

The Devastation Of War

War only leads to more
It is the cause of everything bad
It makes everyone sad
Is there anything else I can add?

There are weapons and blood
Burnt bodies in the wet mud
Killing and dying
This is terrible, they are crying
The soldier holds his gun
He strikes fear everywhere he comes.

Haseeb Ahmad Syed (11)
Stanton School, Milton Keynes

Left Alone

No food, no house
No roof over my head
I've got no bed
To rest my head.

No money, no food
Nothing to eat
No family for me
I am left for dead.

I beg for money
Still nothing to eat
I am on the streets
All alone.
No friend for me
Only a teddy in my hand
I wonder where I am
I forgot school
I forgot the things I love to do.

Samantha Masedza (11)
Stanton School, Milton Keynes

Nothing But Silence

As the cool breeze scatters on the desolate road
When people lie in bed
Death occurs as they close their eyes
Tears fall as the funerals begin
Malaria, viruses and lots more
Affect the poor and even the rich
The way they sway, the way they twitch
So come on and stop this horrible crisis
And the tears will stop in no time
Death is mostly by sickness
That laughs evilly in your body.

Suheub Awale (11)
Stanton School, Milton Keynes

One Solution!

Pollution is horrible
It has one solution
Just put the waste where it belongs
Or it will cause extinction

Pollution is vicious
As you're walking down the street
You smell the awful smell
Of the pollution's stinky feet

It will make you scream
As it melts the ice caps
Losing water for a while
So turn off your taps.

Shannon Griffin (11)
Stanton School, Milton Keynes

Reduce, Reuse, Recycle

My world will stay green
Forever and a day
My world will stay clean
So I never go away
Reduce, reuse, recycle

My world is the best
For saving the planet
My world's better than the rest
Reduce, reuse, recycle

Keep it green and save the world
Look at the signs
And you'll see the world was made for me.

Kayleigh-Louise Wills (11)
Stanton School, Milton Keynes

Why War?

Why use war?
It's a living hell,
People die, people yell.
The fight is pointless,
Death toll rises,
Uses dangerous weapons,
Making a crisis.

Bombs go off without a warning,
People scream,
People mourning,
Bullets are wasted
On innocent men,
But they shoot back, again and again.

Why have war?
It's totally useless,
People end up dying,
It's totally thoughtless.

Ankur Vaghadia (11)
Stanton School, Milton Keynes

Good Or Bad?

The family you always wanted shot and hit to death,
Brothers, sisters, Mum and Dad fade away like a myth.
No food, no water for all the year,
Spent money on a bit of beer.
You're hanging on a piece of string, between life and death,
You can see the life you always wanted shatter into bits.
Your future doesn't look so bright,
Don't think I will sleep tonight.

Ali Ul-Zafar (11)
Stanton School, Milton Keynes

World Of War

War is bad, war is hell
Is it good or bad?
No one can tell
Firing guns at people in sight
Killing people day and night

Evil torture, spilling blood
People fight among the mud
It isn't good, it's wrong and bad
Killing people makes others mad
War is bad, war is wrong.

Stop this now, devastating demise
People die through the blade of a knife
It's wrong, it's cruel, it's worthless too
War is bad, do you think it's true?

George Wilson (11)
Stanton School, Milton Keynes

Riddle

I'm sometimes on the floor,
There's always room for more,
I'm here, I'm there, I'm everywhere,
That's something I'll always share.

If the bins are full,
It's like getting kicked by a bull,
It's never a bore,
As I'm on the greasy floor.

I destroy animals' habitats,
Now will you look at that?
I feel very sad,
It makes me mad,
What am I?

Answer: Litter.

Stephanie Takyi (10)
Stanton School, Milton Keynes

Make The World A Better Place

We could make the world a better place
By always seeing a friendly face.
We could stop arguments before they start
If more people listened to their heart.
We could make the world a greener place
By recycling rubbish it will cause less waste.
We could help countries that are poor
By giving food, clothes and more.
We should not throw rubbish on the floor
And countries should talk to prevent a war.
We could all get on if we only tried
We should tell the truth and not a lie.

Ben Scott (9)
Sundon Park Junior School, Luton

Pollution Needs A Solution

When you look outside what do you see?
Animals and insects, not really;
Fumes and gases more likely.
The danger is extreme,
So use your legs, not your motor,
This pollution needs a solution before it gets too late.
You can start now,
Pick up your litter and recycle when you can,
You can make a difference.

Samantha Thompson (10)
Sundon Park Junior School, Luton

The World

To make the world a better place,
You have to stop fighting over race.
Black and white living together,
Friends together, life would be better.
Stop the starving, feed the hungry,
Send the spare food to feed the hungry.
When disaster strikes, like tsunamis,
Countries should help and send in their armies.
Rebuild the countries who have suffered this fate,
Rehouse these people before it's too late.
My name is Sam and I am nine,
Let's work together for this world of mine.

Samamtha Cox (9)
Sundon Park Junior School, Luton

A Better Place To Be

I'd like to make the world a better place to be
for people to live and breathe,
With more trees and plants and police on the streets
to put us at our ease.
We should recycle and reuse and not just throw away,
think about your rubbish and use it another way.
Be kind to one another
and look out for your sister and brother.
Don't forget to smile at people you may meet,
a smile can make you happy,
so don't walk looking at your feet.

Sophie Little (9)
Sundon Park Junior School, Luton

Pollution Poem

No one be bad,
or everybody will be sad.
No one litter,
or the world won't glitter.
Don't cut down wood
because that wouldn't be good.
When countries go to war,
it makes people poor.
Respect other races
because we all have the same hearts and faces.
Don't say things to be cruel,
being nice is much more cool.
The world is full of pollution,
so let's get together and find a solution.

Ross Grieves (9)
Sundon Park Junior School, Luton

If I Could Change The World

If I could change the world,
What changes would there be?
No rubbish lying around
Or bad drugs for you and me.
If I could change the world,
What changes would I make?
People being nicer,
A lot more give than take.
If I could change the world,
What changes would I try?
Decreasing the pollution,
That is causing the world to die.

Charlotte Rattigan (9)
Sundon Park Junior School, Luton

Litter

Litter is here, litter is there
Litter is everywhere
On the floor, in the trees
I plead for it to be cleared.

Wrappers here, wrappers there
Wrappers everywhere
On the floor, in the trees
I want it to be clean.

Recycle your rubbish when you can
It will be taken away in the big green van
Recycle, recycle all you can
Help the environment whenever you can.

Kyle Perry (10)
Sundon Park Junior School, Luton

Environment

E arth's in trouble
N o more icebergs
V alleys drying up
I t's causing so much pollution
R ainforest destruction
O zone layer getting destroyed
N o more trees
M ore carbon dioxide in the air
E very day the climate changes
N o more animals
T ry to help the Earth.

Regan Cook (9)
Sundon Park Junior School, Luton

To Make The World A Better Place

War, war
There would never be any more.
Screaming, shouting and abuse
Should never ever be in use.
Be good and nice to colour, religion and race
We live together with no disgrace
Kids and youths on the streets
Catch them out before they meet.
Drugs, alcohol and stealing cars
Never good, you'll meet the bars.
Animals, mammals and birds
Please don't hurt us and destroy our homes.
All we want to do is live on this planet
And share it with you.

To make the world a better place
Recite this poem as above.

Sophie Allford-Rowe (9)
Sundon Park Junior School, Luton

If I Could Make The World A Better Place

If I could make the world a better place,
I would change the human race.
No famine, no wars,
No breaking the laws.
With segregation,
Makes the world a bad nation.
No jealousy, no greed,
No hypocrisy.

Destiny-Blu Atkinson (9)
Sundon Park Junior School, Luton

What A Life!

What a life,
The birds singing,
Lions with their young.
They were the good days,
The sweet days,
The gone days.
Men came,
They killed my people,
They hunted my animals,
They burned our houses,
They cut down our trees,
The birds fled,
They have ruined my life.

Luke Chambers (10)
Sundon Park Junior School, Luton

The World

Everyone needs to help
To make the world a better place
Littering, pollution scattered all around
We need to reduce down the big amount
After all we are human beings
Living and seeing
The world go to waste
Even if it is at a slow pace
We are going to destroy the human race
And when we grow old
This will all be gone
And soon there will be no one.

Elisabeth Bunker (10)
Sundon Park Junior School, Luton

Saving The World

If I could change the world,
what changes would there be?
Bullying would stop so people could be free.
In rainforests people shouldn't cut down trees
because animals live in them, including bees.
Recycle paper, plastic and tin
and always remember to put them in the correct bins.
Protect the ozone as if it's your own.

Ellisse-Renais Clarke (9)
Sundon Park Junior School, Luton

Fantastic Planet Earth

Planet Earth is just fantastic,
Let's get rid of all the plastic.
Recycle is best, put it to the test,
Then this country will be the best.
Try to walk, not to use the car,
We can have fresh air to breathe.
If we don't recycle glass, plastic and paper, to name a few . . .
The world will be a worse place for me and you to live in.

Bethany Ruck (9)
Sundon Park Junior School, Luton

Making The World A Better Place

You can make the world a better place,
No matter what your colour, religion or race.
By working together and thinking of other people's needs,
As most of the trouble is through greed.
If we all do something small by recycling rubbish
And walking to school - this would help us all.

Matthew Wajda (9)
Sundon Park Junior School, Luton

Our World

What are we doing
to this world of ours?
Why don't we stop
using our cars?
The cars are getting bigger
and it's starting to trigger
bad changes in the weather,
so why don't we get together
and look after our world?

Aidan Drury (9)
Sundon Park Junior School, Luton

Rubbish

Rubbish, rubbish everywhere,
People just don't seem to care.

Put it in the bin,
Or it is a sin.

Litter, litter on the ground,
Everywhere you look around.

It's not nice, it's not fair,
People just don't seem to care.

Sophie Mullings (10)
Sundon Park Junior School, Luton

Litter

L et's all help to save the planet
I ntelligence is not needed
T here are three tips to follow:
T ry to buy recyclable items
E ncourage others to reuse items
R educe, reuse and recycle.

Ryan O'Reilly (10)
Sundon Park Junior School, Luton

If I Could Change The World

If I could change the world, what changes would there be?
I'd stop the wars, the fighting and we'd live in harmony.
There would be no knives or guns and gangs involved in crime,
No innocent people getting hurt, we'd feel safe all the time.
I'd encourage recycling to save our lovely Earth,
Saving trees and animals, I'd make people see their worth.
I'd educate the people in countries rich and poor,
I'd feed and vaccinate them so illness was no more.
So now I'll go and start to make the world a better place,
By doing what I can to help with a smile on my face.

Luke Williams (8)
Sundon Park Junior School, Luton

If We . . .

If we didn't have a bath and all had a shower,
We would use less water and save more power.
If we all took the trouble to recycle more,
Use the bins provided, we would have cleaner floors.
If we used our legs more, instead of a car,
We would get more exercise which is better by far.
Be nicer to people and fight a lot less,
The world would be better and not in a mess.
Let's try together, as one big race,
Then this world would be a better place.

Danielle Fortune (9)
Sundon Park Junior School, Luton

Problems On Earth

Electricity power being so sour to the Earth,
Everything is using it - including the Blackpool Tower!
This is one problem!
Stations vomiting smoke into the air,
Does anyone care?
Global warming.

Problems, problems everywhere you go,
The problems everyone has caused.
Lazy world being so cruel to the Earth,
Filling it up like a junkyard, no one is bothered.
This is one problem!
Recycling can help save energy.
Does anyone care?
Global warming.

Problems, problems everywhere you go,
The problems everyone has caused.
Polluting world being so nasty to the Earth,
Releasing CO_2 into the air to warm it, vehicle-filled roads.
This is one problem!
Take public transport, use your feet or bike.
Does anyone care?
Global warming.

Crystal Bonnar (11) & Kara Watkin
Welland Primary School, Peterborough

Danger

D o you care about the world? Didn't think so.
A ggressively you pollute the Earth.
N ervously the Earth trembles with fear.
G o to the bottle bank and put your bottles
   where they should be - *recycle*.
E xhaust pipes pollute the atmosphere - *pollution*.
R esponsibility is yours.

Jasmine May House (11)
Welland Primary School, Peterborough

Whale Poem

Monstrous, dark waves crash,
Another innocent victim to its power.
Burning like a snake's bite,
Like an ant against a foot.
The victim has no chance against the oil-wanting humans.
Big friendly giant sings peacefully, swings gracefully,
Getting closer to the wall of death.
Sudden suffering under the moonlight,
Listen to the whale's sad cry as it lies tragically poisoned
                                          under the black sky.
Washed up to the shore,
She lives no more,
Who cares? The oil is needed!

Chloe Nickelson (10) & Shannon Mouatt (11)
Welland Primary School, Peterborough

Litter, Litter

Litter, litter everywhere
Some is here and some is there
To make our planet a better place
Pick up your litter just throw it in the bin
Litter, litter
Why do you spread disease?

Awais Riaz (8)
William Austin Junior School, Luton

Recycle, Recycle

Recycle, recycle, litter everywhere
Recycle, recycle, put your litter in the bin.
Litter, litter, recycle your cans into the recycle bin.
The world will be a mess if you don't recycle every day.
The enormous world of recycling.

Habibur Rahman (9)
William Austin Junior School, Luton

Recycling

R ecycling it
E xcept from binning it
C are for the environment
Y our life is in your hands
C ycle your life
L ife, life, life
I n your hands
N ow recycle
G o and recycle.

Keira Chew (9)
William Austin Junior School, Luton

Changing The World

Litter flows when you make mess.
Being homeless with sickness to die with.
Rainforests cut because of waste.
Diseases around us, nowhere to hide.
War goes on in dangerous places around.
And animals are made extinct because of hunting.
Remember the 3 Rs and stop polluting.
Reduce, reuse, recycle!

Sumayyah Iqbal (9)
William Austin Junior School, Luton

Stop Pollution

Never litter,
Make our planet glitter,
Help us clean the town,
Before we let the government down.

Sabia Shafiq (9)
William Austin Junior School, Luton

Need An Island In The Sea

Need an island in the sea,
away from you, away from me,
beyond the waves, beyond the wind,
beyond the world that we live in.
Under skies of shining stars,
away from light and noisy cars.
A place for me, a place for you,
an Earth that's green, a sky that's blue.
A place for you, a place for me,
an open sky and light blue sea.
With dreams as solid as the ground,
a place like this I think I've found,
a happy place.

Arooj Khan (9)
William Austin Junior School, Luton

What Is Going On?

You need to start recycling,
to save the world right here.
If you don't start recycling,
destruction is near.
The world is near the end,
you really should start now,
but all you have to answer
is the question - how?
I will tell you how to do it,
if you think it's true,
you have to start recycling,
to make the world brand new.

Georgia Webster (9)
William Austin Junior School, Luton

Look After Your Home

Look after your home
Look after your planet
Made of granite
Look after your home
And your globe
Treat it nicely
And most likely
You're becoming
A true friend
To the end
But to help -
Recycle
It's worth it
Give birth to it.

So if you want to keep the world concave
You'd better behave.

Chloe Walker (9)
William Austin Junior School, Luton

Caring For The Environment

Recycle, recycle all your mess,
Because the waste would be less.

Recycle, recycle your cans and tins,
Then there would be no use for black bins.

Recycle, recycle all your plastic,
That would make the world fantastic.

Recycle, recycle all your metal,
From your toaster to your kettle.

Recycle, recycle, why don't you?
I'm doing it too!

Alina Ali (8)
William Austin Junior School, Luton

Young Writers Information

We hope you have enjoyed reading this book - and that you will continue to enjoy it in the coming years.

If you like reading and writing poetry drop us a line, or give us a call, and we'll send you a free information pack.

Alternatively if you would like to order further copies of this book or any of our other titles, then please give us a call or log onto our website at www.youngwriters.co.uk

**Young Writers Information
Remus House
Coltsfoot Drive
Peterborough
PE2 9JX**

(01733) 890066